Ultimate
IQ Tests

Ultimate IQ Tests

1,000 practice test questions to boost your brain power

Philip Carter and Ken Russell

KOGAN
PAGE

London and Philadelphia

Publisher's note

Every possible effort has been made to ensure that the information contained in this book is accurate at the time of going to press, and the publishers and authors cannot accept responsibility for any errors or omissions, however caused. No responsibility for loss or damage occasioned to any person acting, or refraining from action, as a result of the material in this publication can be accepted by the editor, the publisher or any of the authors.

Tests included in this book have previously been included in *The Times Book of IQ Tests: Book 1* (2001), *The Times Book of IQ Tests: Book 3* (2003) and *The Times Book of IQ Tests: Book 5* (2005) published by Kogan Page.

First published in Great Britain and the United States in 2006 as *The Ultimate IQ Test Book* by Kogan Page Limited.
Reissued in 2009 as *Ultimate IQ Tests*

120 Pentonville Road   525 South 4th Street, #241
London N1 9JN   Philadelphia PA 19147
United Kingdom   USA
www.koganpage.com

© Phillip Carter and Ken Russell, 2006, 2009

The right of Phillip Carter and Ken Russell to be identified as the authors of this work has been asserted by them in accordance with the Copyright, Designs and Patents Act 1988.

ISBN 978 0 7494 5309 1

British Library Cataloguing-in-Publication Data

A CIP record for this book is available from the British Library.

Library of Congress Cataloging-in-Publication Data
Carter, Philip.
  Ultimate IQ tests : 1000 practice test questions to boost your brain power / Philip Carter and Ken Russell.
        p. cm.
  Includes bibliographical references and index.
  ISBN 978-0-7494-5309-1 (alk. paper)
1. Intellect. 2. Self-evaluation. I. Russell, Kenneth A., II. Title
  BF31.3.C373 2008
  153.9'3--dc22

                                          200803

Typeset by Saxon Graphics Ltd, Derby
Printed and bound in India by Replika Press Pvt Ltd

Contents

Introduction   1

Test 1: Questions   5
Test 2: Questions   16
Test 3: Questions   27
Test 4: Questions   38
Test 5: Questions   47
Test 6: Questions   57
Test 7: Questions   68
Test 8: Questions   80
Test 9: Questions   90
Test 10: Questions   100
Test 11: Questions   110
Test 12: Questions   121
Test 13: Questions   131
Test 14: Questions   142
Test 15: Questions   153
Test 16: Questions   164
Test 17: Questions   175
Test 18: Questions   188
Test 19: Questions   200
Test 20: Questions   212
Test 21: Questions   224
Test 22: Questions   236
Test 23: Questions   246
Test 24: Questions   258
Test 25: Questions   269

Answers and explanations   279

Introduction

Of the different methods that purport to measure intelligence, the most famous is the IQ (Intelligence Quotient) test, which is a standardized test designed to measure human intelligence as distinct from attainments.

Intelligence quotient is an age-related measure of intelligence level. The word quotient means the result of dividing one quantity by another, and one definition of intelligence is mental ability or quickness of mind.

Usually, IQ tests consist of a graded series of tasks, each of which has been standardized with a large representative population of individuals in order to establish an average IQ of 100 for each test.

It is generally accepted that a person's mental ability develops at a constant rate until about the age of 13, after which development has been shown to slow down, and beyond the age of 18 little or no improvement is found.

When the IQ of a child is measured, the subject attempts an IQ test that has been standardized, with an average score recorded for each age group. Thus a 10-year-old child who scored the result that would be expected of a 12-year-old would have an IQ of 120, or 12/10 × 100:

$$\frac{\text{mental age}\,(12)}{\text{chronological age}\,(10)} \times 100 = 120 \text{ IQ}$$

Because after the age of 18 little or no improvement is found, adults have to be judged on an IQ test whose average score is 100, and the results graded above and below this norm according to known test scores.

Like so many distributions found in nature, the distribution of IQ takes the form of a fairly regular bell curve (see Figure 0.1 overleaf) in which the average score is 100 and similar proportions occur both above and below this norm.

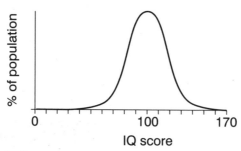

Figure 0.1   The bell curve

There are a number of different types of intelligence tests, for example Cattell, Stanford-Binet and Wechsler, and each has its own different scales of intelligence.

The Stanford-Binet is heavily weighted with questions involving verbal abilities and is widely used in the United States. The Weschler scales consist of two separate verbal and performance sub-scales each with its own IQ rating. On the Stanford-Binet scale half the population fall between 90 and 110 IQ, half of them above 100 and half of them below; 25 per cent score above 110; 11 per cent above 120; 3 per cent above 130 and 0.6 per cent above 140. At the other end of the scale the same kind of proportion occurs.

Although it is IQ tests that we are specifically concerned with in this book it should be pointed out that IQ tests are just one part of what is generally referred to as psychometric testing. Such test content may be addressed to almost any aspect of our intellectual or emotional make-up, including personality, attitude, intelligence or emotion. Psychometric tests are basically tools used for measuring the mind; the word metric means *measure* and the word psycho means *mind*. There are two types of psychometric tests that are usually used in tandem by employers. These are aptitude tests, which assess your abilities, and personality questionnaires, which assess your character and personality.

Aptitude tests are also known as cognitive, ability or intelligence (IQ) tests. Such tests are designed to test your ability to comprehend quickly under strictly timed conditions. Cognition may be broadly defined as knowing, perceiving and thinking and it is studied by psychologists because it reveals the extent of a person's ability to think.

There are many different types of tests. However, a typical test might consist of three sections each testing a different ability, usually comprising verbal reasoning, numerical ability and diagrammatic, or spatial, reasoning. In order to give you the opportunity to practise all types of questions that you are likely to encounter in actual IQ tests, the tests that have been compiled for this book are multi-discipline and include a mix of verbal, numerical and diagrammatic questions, as well as additional questions involving logical thought processes as well as a degree of lateral thinking.

In the past 25 years psychometric testing has been brought into widespread use in industry because of the need for employers to ensure they place the right people in the right job at the outset. One of the main reasons for this is the high cost of errors in today's world of tight budgets and reduced profit margins. To recruit a new member of staff an employer has to advertise, consider each application, reduce the applicants to a shortlist, interview and then train the successful applicant. If the wrong hiring choice has been made, then the whole expensive process has to be repeated.

It is important that such tests are evaluated in tandem with each other. If a person scores well on an aptitude test it does not necessarily mean that they will be suited to the job: whilst you may be good at doing something, you may dislike it intensely, and success in most tasks is heavily dependent on your personal qualities and your attitude.

Although it is generally accepted that a person's IQ remains constant throughout life and therefore it is not possible to increase your actual IQ, it is possible to improve your performance on IQ tests by practising the many different types of question and learning to recognize the recurring themes.

Besides their uses in improving one's performance on IQ tests, practice on the type of questions contained in this book has the added advantage of exercising the brain. Our brains need exercise and care in the same way as other parts of the body. We eat the right foods to keep our heart healthy, we moisturise our skin to keep it from drying out and, just as gymnasts strive to increase their performance at whatever level they are competing by means of punishing training schedules and refinement of technique, there are exercises, or mental gymnastics, we can do to increase the performance of our brains and enhance quickness of thought.

Many people still have the outdated belief that there is little they can do to improve the brain they are born with and that brain cells continually degenerate with age: but, in fact, our brain cells continually develop new and stronger connections and adult brains can grow new cells irrespective of age.

The main thing is to use your brain continually. For example, the more we practise at tests of verbal aptitude the more we increase our ability to understand the meaning of words and use them effectively; the more we practise at maths the more confident we become when working with numbers, the better our ability to perform arithmetic operations accurately, and the quicker we become at performing these operations; and the more we practise our ability to move our fingers and manipulate small objects the more dextrous we become at operations involving this type of aptitude, and the quicker we become at performing them accurately.

The tests that follow have been compiled for this book and are not, therefore, standardized, so an actual IQ assessment cannot be given. However, a guide to assessing your performance for each test is provided below as well as a cumulative guide for your overall performance on all 25 tests.

A time limit of 90 minutes is allowed for each test. The correct answers are given at the end of the book, and you should award yourself one point for each completely correct answer. Calculators may be used to assist with solving numerical questions if preferred.

Use the following table to assess your performance in each of the 25 tests:

Score	Rating
36–40	Exceptional
31–35	Excellent
25–30	Very good
19–24	Good
14–18	Average

Questions

1. 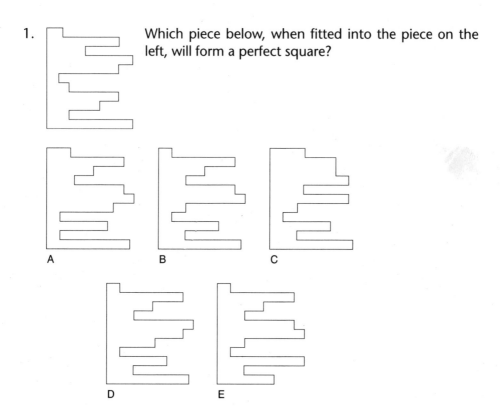 Which piece below, when fitted into the piece on the left, will form a perfect square?

2. Which word in brackets is most opposite to the word in capitals?

    PROSCRIBE (allow, stifle, promote, verify, indict)

3. 0, 1, 2, 4, 6, 9, 12, 16, ?

    What number should replace the question mark?

4. Which number is the odd one out?

    9678 4572 5261 5133 3527 6895 7768

5. Isotherm is to temperature as isobar is to: atmosphere, wind, pressure, latitude, current

6.

1	2	4	7
4	?	7	10
6	?	?	12
7	8	10	?

Which is the missing section?

A

B

C

D

7. Which is the odd one out?

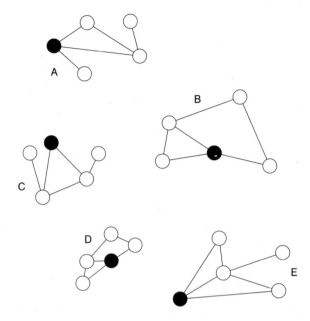

8. Identify two words (one from each set of brackets) that have a connection (analogy) with the words in capitals and relate to them in the same way.

   GRAM (energy, weight, scales)

   KNOT (water, rope, speed)

9.

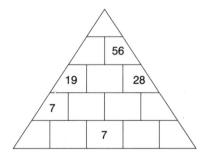

Each number in the pyramid is the sum of the two numbers immediately below it. Fill in the pyramid with the missing numbers.

10. Which is the odd one out?

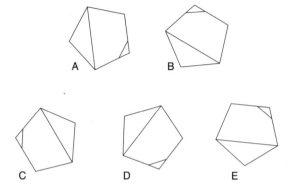

11. How many minutes is it before 12 noon, if 48 minutes ago it was twice as many minutes past 9 am?

12. Complete the five words below in such a way that the two letters that end the first word also start the second word, and the two letters that end the second word also start the third word etc. The same two letters that end the fifth word also start the first word, to complete the cycle.

    ** IV **

    ** OT **

    ** IC **

    ** NG **

    ** RA **

13. Which is the odd one out?

    heptagon, triangle, hexagon, cube, pentagon

14. Switch A turns lights 1 and 2 on/off or off/on

    Switch B turns lights 2 and 4 on/off or off/on

    Switch C turns lights 1 and 3 on/off or off/on

     = ON

     = OFF

    Switches C, A and B are thrown in turn with the result that Figure 1 turns into Figure 2. Which switch does not work at all?

    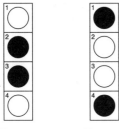

    Figure 1   Figure 2

15.

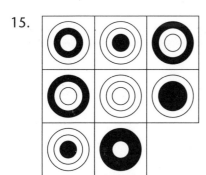

    Which is the missing tile?

    A   B   C   D   E

16. Which word in brackets is closest in meaning to the word in capitals?

    BRUNT (dull, edifice, impact, tawny, nonsense)

17. Which of the following is not an anagram of a type of food?

PAST EIGHT

I CAN ROAM

WIN BOAR

CAN PEAK

COOL CHEAT

18.

What number should replace the question mark?

19.

N	O	I	
A	R	O	S
L		F	E

Work from square to adjacent square horizontally or vertically (but not diagonally) to spell out a 12-letter word. You must find the starting point, and provide the missing letters.

20. How many lines appear below?

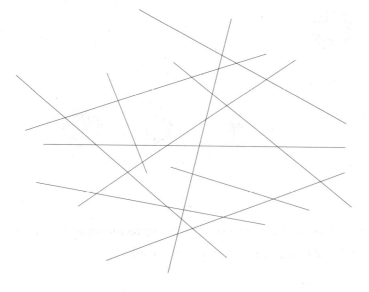

21.

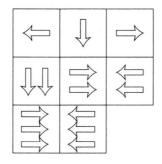

Which is the missing tile?

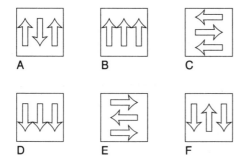

22. 6⅞, 2⁹/₁₆, 5⅝, 3³/₁₆, 4³/₈, ?

What number should replace the question mark?

23.

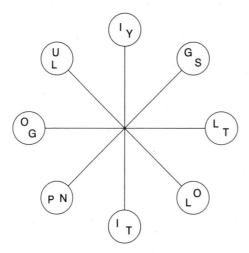

Work clockwise round the circles to spell out two eight-letter words that are synonyms. Each word commences in a different circle, and you must find the starting point of each. Every letter is used once each and all letters are consecutive.

24. 10, 30, 32, 96, 98, 294, 296, ?, ?
    What two numbers should replace the question marks?

25. able, rot, son, king
    Which word below shares a common feature with all the words above?
    line, sit, take, hope, night

26. Identify two words (one from each set of brackets) that have a connection (analogy) with the words in capitals and relate to them in the same way.
    SEA (wet, swimmer, ship)
    SNOW (mountain, ice, skier)

27. Which word meaning LOCALITY becomes a word meaning TEMPO when a letter is removed?

28. Alf has four times as many as Jim, and Jim has three times as many as Sid. Altogether they have 192.
    How many has each?

29. Which is the only one of the following that is not an anagram of a word meaning *out of this world*?
    flow under
    sexed Utah
    enviable blue
    icier blend

30. A man has 53 socks in his drawer: 21 identical blue, 15 identical black and 17 identical red. The lights are fused and he is completely in the dark. How many socks must he take out to make 100 per cent certain he has a pair of black socks?

31.

    Draw the missing figure in the above sequence.

32. How many minutes is it before 12 noon if nine minutes ago it was twice as many minutes past 10 am?

33. Which two words are closest in meaning?
    conclave, medley, theme, conglomeration, dissertation, augury

34. broke rage prose cute dared   ?
    Which word is missing?
    palm hymn evil snow take

35. Find *five* consecutive numbers below that total 22.
    7 3 9 6 4 1 3 7 9 3 5 4 1 7 6 5

36.
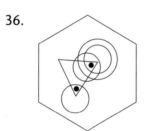

    To which hexagon below can a dot be added so that both dots then meet the same conditions as the two dots in the hexagon above?

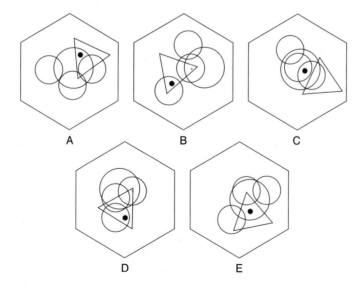

37. Find two words (4, 6) in this diagram. Letters are traced across the circle by chords. If the next letter is four letters or less away it will be found by tracing around the circumference. Clue: free flight.

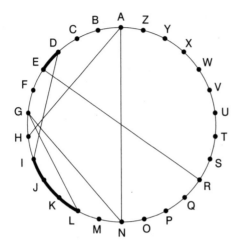

38.

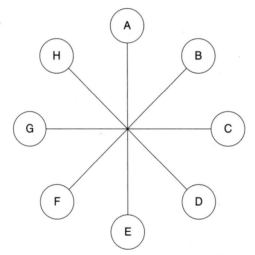

What letter is directly opposite the letter that is two letters away clock-wise from the letter that is directly opposite the letter E?

39.

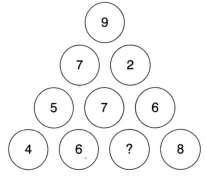

What number should replace the question mark?

40.

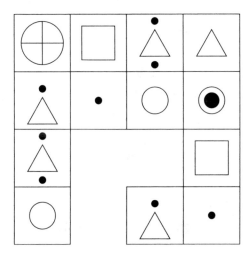

Which is the missing section?

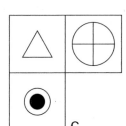

A

B

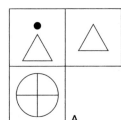

C

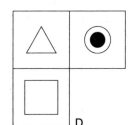

D

1.

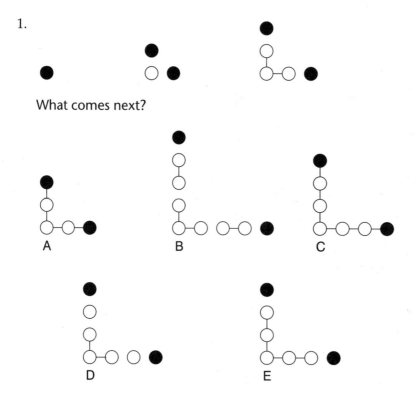

What comes next?

2. Which four-letter word, when placed in the brackets, will complete a word on the left and start another word on the right?

RAM (****) RIDGE

3.

20	22	19	21
17	19	16	?
19	21	?	20
16	18	15	?

Which is the missing section?

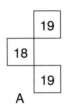 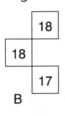 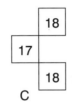 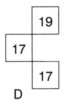

A B C D

4. ligno- is to wood as vitro- is to wool, glass, stone, water, paper?

5.

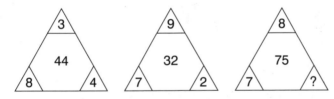

What number should replace the question mark?

6. Solve the anagrams to find a well-known saying. The number of letters in each word is shown.

(**** ** ********)(**** *******)

(asserting craft)(hint of antic)

7.

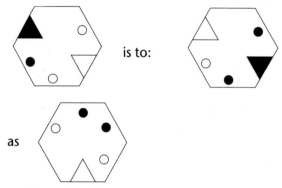

is to:

as

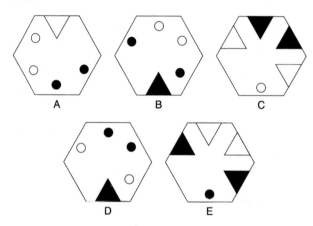

is to:

8. 0, 4, 2, 6, 3, 7, 3.5, ?

What number should replace the question mark?

9. Identify two words (one from each set of brackets) that have a connection (analogy) with the words in capitals and relate to them in the same way.

LONGITUDE (degree, tropics, meridian)

LATITUDE (parallel, line, equinox)

10.

5	2	3	10
6	4	1	11
1	9	?	12
12	?	6	?

Which is the missing section?

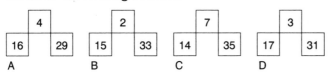

A   B   C   D

11. Which word in brackets is closest in meaning to the word in capitals?
MONITOR (observe, order, meddle, intrude, conclude)

12.

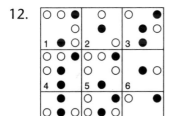

Looking at lines across and down, if the first two tiles are combined to produce the third tile, with the exception that like symbols are cancelled out, which of the above tiles is incorrect, and with which of the tiles below should it be replaced?

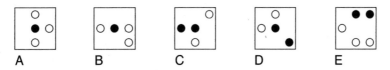

A   B   C   D   E

13. Which two words are most opposite in meaning?
liberty, frivolity, chastity, sobriety, irrationality, polarity

14.

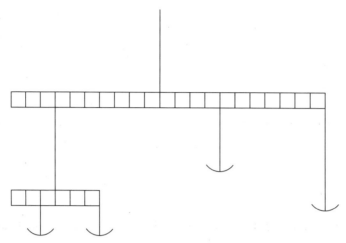

Insert four weights of 2 units, 3 units, 4 units and 6 units respectively so that the scales balance perfectly.

15. The following clue leads to which pair of rhyming words?

measure bulk of grass fodder

16.

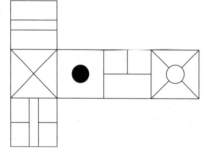

When the above is folded to form a cube, which is the only one of the following that *can* be produced?

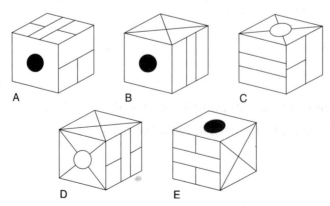

17. Which is the odd one out?

    femur, mandible, fibula, tibia, patella

18. My watch was correct at noon, after which it started to lose 17 minutes per hour until six hours ago it stopped completely. It now shows the time as 2.52 pm. What time is it now?

19.

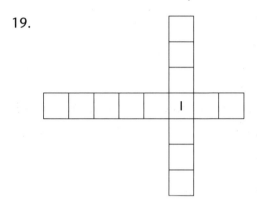

Insert all the letters of the phrase UNSPOILT LOCAL into the remaining blank spaces once each only, to produce two words that form a phrase. Clue: things are not always what they appear.

20.

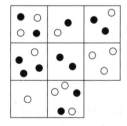

Which is the missing tile?

A   B   C   D   E

21.

What comes next?

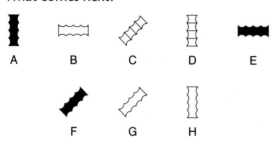

22. dopiness, uncloaking, dishwasher

Which word below has a feature in common with all the words above?

gallant, crossfire, whirlwind, assault

23. 1, 101, 15, 4, 29, –93, 43, –190, ?

What number should replace the question mark?

24.

A	B	C	D	E	
F	G	H	I	J	
K	L	M	N	O	
P	Q	R	S	T	
U	V	W	X	Y	Z

What letter is two letters above the letter two letters to the left of the letter immediately above the letter three letters to the right of the letter Q?

25. 15, 5, 8, 24, 21, 7, 10, 30, ?, ?, ?, 36, 33

What three numbers are missing?

26.

Which shield below has most in common with the shield above?

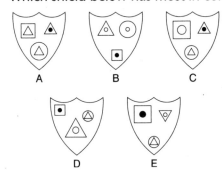

A   B   C

D   E

27. Using the four letters below only, create a seven-letter word.

UMNI

28.

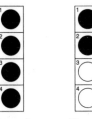

What number should replace the question mark?

29. Switch A turns lights 1 and 2 on/off or off/on
    Switch B turns lights 2 and 4 on/off or off/on
    Switch C turns lights 1 and 3 on/off or off/on
    Switch D turns lights 3 and 4 on/off or off/on

    ● = ON

    ○ = OFF

Switches D, C, A and B are thrown in turn with the result that Figure 1 turns into Figure 2. Which switch does not work at all?

Figure 1   Figure 2

30. Which word in brackets is closest in meaning to the word in capitals?

    FUSE (muzzle, explode, coalesce, immobilize, tighten)

31.

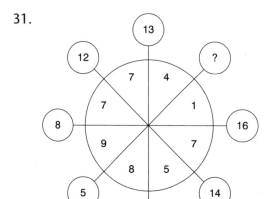

    What number should replace the question mark?

32.

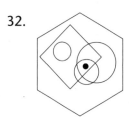

    To which hexagon below can a dot be added so that it then meets the same conditions as in the hexagon above?

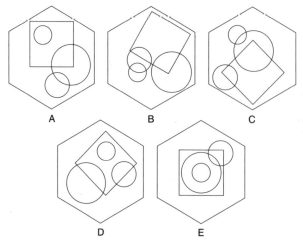

33. You have 59 cubic blocks. What is the minimum number that needs to be taken away in order to construct a solid cube with none left over?

34. What word meaning DEDUCE becomes a word meaning PROPEL when a letter is removed?

35.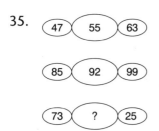

What number should replace the question mark?

36. What is the longest word in the English language that can be produced from the set of letters below? Letters may only be used once in the word produced.

FEUMOPXCTW

37.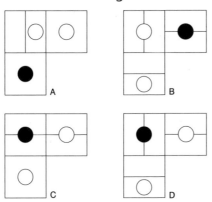

Which is the missing section?

38.

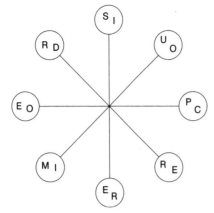

Work clockwise round the circles to spell out two eight-letter words that are antonyms. Each word commences in a different circle, and you must find the starting point of each. Every letter is used once each and all letters are consecutive.

39.

What number should replace the question mark?

40.

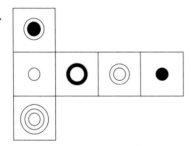

When the above is folded to form a cube, which is the only one of the following that *can* be produced?

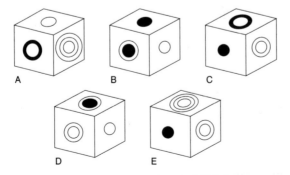

A   B   C

D   E

Questions

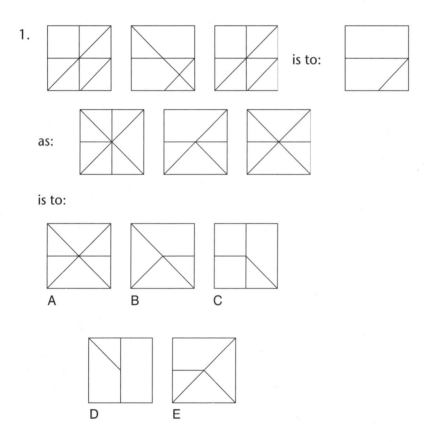

1.

is to:

as:

is to:

A   B   C

D   E

2. Which is the odd one out?

cymbal, marimba, vibraphone, trombone, glockenspiel

3. stationary, less, stationery, principal, fewer, principle

   Place the words above alongside their correct definition below:

   head of school
   fundamental truth
   standing still
   writing materials
   smaller in amount
   smaller in number

4. Which is the odd number out?

   462 683 385 198 253 781 594

5. PURE AS TUFT is an anagram of which two words that are opposite in meaning?

6.

A	B	C	D	E
F	G	H	I	J
K	L	M	N	O
P	Q	R	S	T
U	V	W	X	Y

Z

Which letter is midway between the letter two letters below the letter immediately to the left of the letter G, and the letter three letters above the letter immediately to the right of the letter V?

7.

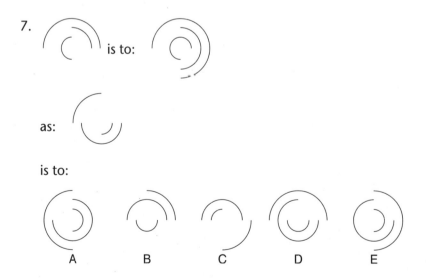

8.

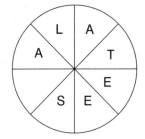 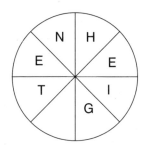

Complete two eight-letter words, one in each circle, and both reading clockwise. The words are synonyms. You must find the starting points and provide the missing letters.

9. 1, 50, 6, 45, 11, 40, 16, 35, 21, ?, ?

Which numbers should replace the question marks?

10. Arrange the words below into alphabetical order.

acescence, acetamide, acerbated, acetified, acellular, acescency, acetabula, acerbates

11.

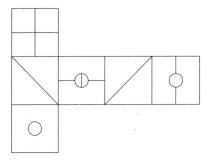

When the above is folded to form a cube, which is the only one of the following that *can* be produced?

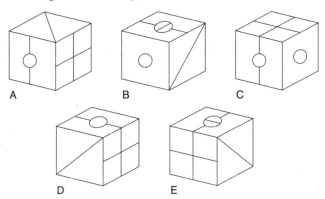

12.

3	9	1	2	8	3
9	?	?	2	1	9
1	?	?	3	9	1
2	1	9	3	8	2
8	3	9	1	2	8
3	8	2	1	9	3

Which is the missing section?

8	3
8	2

A

3	8
2	8

B

8	2
8	3

C

2	8
3	8

D

13. Solve the anagram in brackets to correctly complete the quotation with a 10-letter word.

'The difference between golf and (torn veg men) is that in golf you cannot improve your lie' *George Deukmejian*

14.

Which shield should replace the question mark?

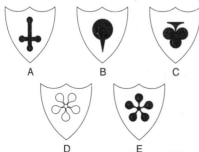

15.

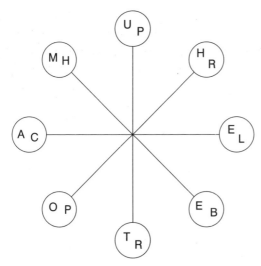

Take one letter from each circle in turn and using each letter once only find two eight-letter words that are similar in meaning. Both words read clockwise and each starts in a different circle.

16. What letters should replace the question marks?

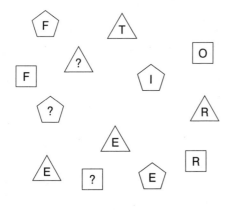

17.

	7				2				5	
9	2	8		7	8	4		6	?	9

What number should replace the question mark?

18. bizarre is to outlandish as eccentric is to: eerie, quirky, esoteric, weird, curious

19. On taking delivery of a consignment of eggs the market stall owner was furious to find that several were cracked. In fact, on counting them up in order to assess the damage he found that 72 were cracked, which was 12 per cent of the total consignment. How many eggs in total were in the consignment?

20.

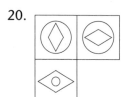

Which is the missing tile?

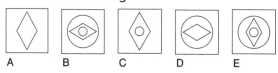

A   B   C   D   E

21. MTD is to PXB as FRJ is to?

22. A B C D E F G H

What letter is two letters to the left of the letter immediately to the right of the letter three letters to the right of the letter A?

23.

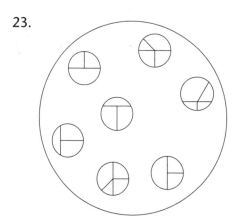

Which circle below should be placed in the large circle above?

A   B   C   D   E

24. Using the five letters below only, create a nine-letter word.

    LOPER

25. 16, 23, 19, 19, 22, 15, 25, ?

    What number should replace the question mark?

26. Simplify:

    $$\frac{14}{55} \div \frac{56}{77}$$

    as the lowest fraction.

27.

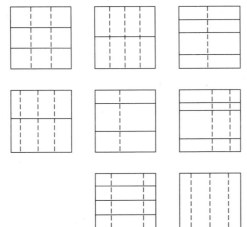

    Which is the missing box?

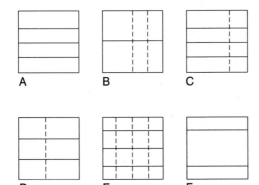

28. Which word in brackets is most opposite in meaning to the word in capitals?

    PLAUSIBLE (appropriate, improbable, clichéd, artificial, distasteful)

29. The cost of an identical three-course lunch for four people was £56.00. The main course cost twice as much as the sweet and the sweet cost twice as much as the starter. How much did the main course cost per person?

30. aplomb, dodge, graph, jerk, ?

    What comes next?

    laugh, maroon, link, nickel, midnight

31.

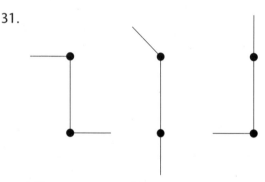

    What comes next?

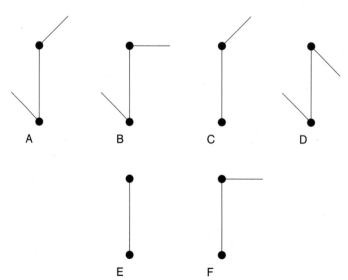

32.

			14	
	22			
			34	
41				
		53		?

What number should replace the question mark?

33. OVATE GNOME is an anagram of which familiar phrase (3, 1, 4, 2)?
Clue: make haste.

34.

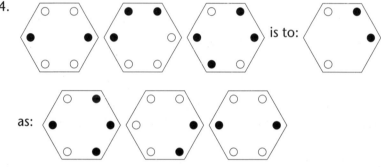

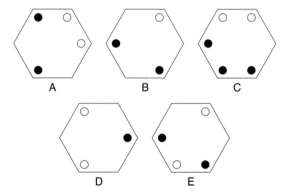

35.

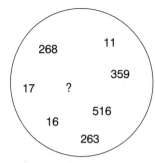

268   11

359

17   ?

516

16

263

What number should replace the question mark?

36.

R	I	N		
T	O	G		
N	S	A	S	D
	A	T	E	
	T	C	H	

Find the starting point and work from letter to adjacent letter vertically, horizontally and diagonally to spell out a 17-letter phrase (2, 7, 8).

37.

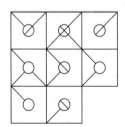

Which is the missing tile?

A   B   C   D   E   F

38.

At each stage the black dot moves three corners clockwise and the white dot moves four corners anticlockwise. After how many stages will both dots be together in the same corner?

39.
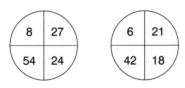

A	A	S	G	P	A	H	A	M
R	S	E	E	I	I	U	G	A
*	*	*	*	*	*	*	*	*

The name of which reptile can be placed on the bottom row to complete nine three-letter words reading downwards?

40.

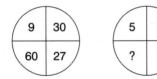

8	27
54	24

6	21
42	18

9	30
60	27

5	?
?	?

What numbers should replace the question marks?

1.

What comes next?

A

B

C

D

E

2. 100, 97.4, 94.8, ?, 89.6, 87

What number should replace the question mark?

3.

E	A	D
		I
P	A	

Start at one of the four corner letters and spiral clockwise round the perimeter, finishing at the centre letter to spell out a nine-letter word. You must provide the missing letters.

4. Which number is the odd one out?

   9654 4832 5945 7642 7963 8216 3649

5. Which two words are closest in meaning?

   qualified, practicable, puissant, feasible, mundane, fine

6. Identify two words (one from each set of brackets) that have a connection (analogy) with the words in capitals and relate to them in the same way.

   FIRST (second, next, last)

   PENULTIMATE (last, third, previous)

7. Find five consecutive numbers below that total 23.

   6 2 9 3 4 7 2 9 3 2 6 4 9 1 2

8.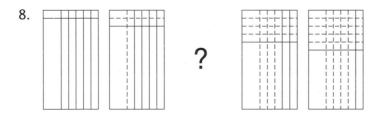

   Draw the missing figure in the above sequence.

9. Which word in brackets is most opposite to the word in capitals?

   SLEEK (sordid, unimaginative, disorderly, dishevelled, oblique)

10.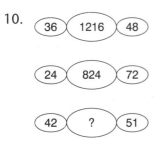

    What number should replace the question mark?

11. Change one letter only in each of the words below to produce a familiar phrase.

    AND FEEL SO TIE WIRE

12. Which is the odd one out?

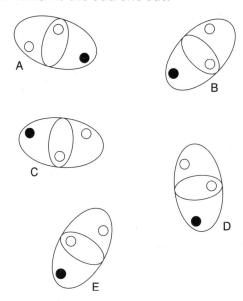

13. Which is the odd one out?

trivet, tributary, triptych, trident, triad

14.

	5	
2	3	8
	11	

	9	
4	5	14
	19	

	13	
6	?	20
	27	

What number should replace the question mark?

15. 5862 is to 714
and 3498 is to 1113
and 9516 is to 156
therefore 8257 is to ?

16.

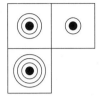

Which is the missing tile?

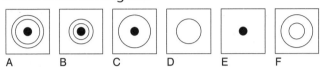

17. mohair is to wool as shantung is to: silk, cotton, linen, nylon, fabric

18.

Place the numbers 1–6 into the circles, one number per circle, so that: the sum of the numbers 4 and 1, and all the numbers between them total 12; the sum of the numbers 4 and 6, and all the numbers between them total 21; the sum of the numbers 2 and 1, and all the numbers between them total 8.

19. If meat in a river (3 in 6) is T(HAM)ES, can you find a monkey in a tall building (3 in 10)?

20.

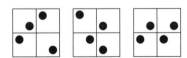

What comes next in the above sequence?

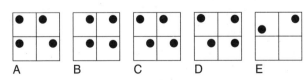

21.

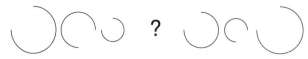

Which arc is missing?

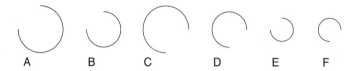

A   B   C   D   E   F

22. Which four bits can be joined together to form two words that have opposite meanings?

ERT, UCE, DES, END, EXP, EAR, AND, SIP, RED, GOS

23.

7	10	13	16
9	12	?	18
11	?	?	20
13	16	19	22

Which is the missing section?

	16
15	18

A

	15
15	18

B

	15
14	17

C

	16
14	17

D

24. Identify two words that sound alike but are spelled differently, which mean:

a straight line connecting two points on a curve
rope

25. Find the ages of Mary, George, Alice, Claire and Stephen if:

Mary + George = 33 years between them
Alice + Claire = 95 years between them
Stephen + Mary = 72 years between them
Mary + Claire = 87 years between them
Stephen + George = 73 years between them

26.
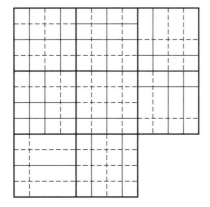

Which is the missing tile?

A   B   C

D   E

27. Using the four letters below only, create a seven-letter word.

CILT

28. 53 (3) 59
92 (4) 98
34 (2) 38
71 (?) 79

What number should replace the question mark?

29.

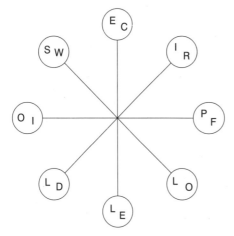

Work clockwise round the circles to spell out two eight-letter words that are synonyms. Each word commences in a different circle, and you must find the starting point of each. Every letter is used once each and all letters are consecutive.

30. 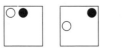 **?**

Draw the missing figure in the above sequence.

31. abashed, derail, little, ?

What comes next?

mellow, entail, leader, elicit, status

32. Produce an eight-letter word by joining together two of these four-letter sets.

cred, agon, lues, once, deva, some, come, pent

33.

20	14	12	24	33
3	10	16	15	18
17	7	4	8	6
5	1	9	30	36
39	21	13	2	11

What number is three places away from itself plus three, two places away from itself multiplied by two, two places away from itself less four and two places away from itself divided by three?

34. 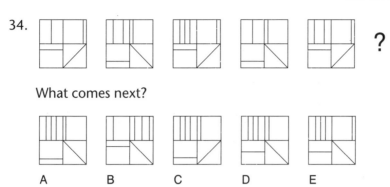 ?

What comes next?

A B C D E

35.

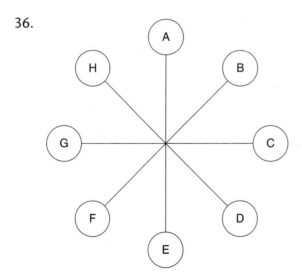

What percentage of the figure is shaded?

36.

What letter is two letters away clockwise from the letter that is directly opposite the letter three letters away anticlockwise from the letter C?

37.

B	E	R
I	E	
	T	A

Spiral clockwise round the perimeter and finish at the centre square to spell out a nine-letter word. You must find the starting point and provide the missing letters.

38. What is one-third of one-quarter of one-fifth of one-half of 120?

39.

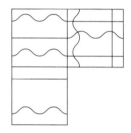

Which is the missing tile?

  A   B   C

       D   E

40.

1	10	7	16
28	19	22	13
25	34	31	40
?	43	46	37

What number should replace the question mark?

Questions

1. Which is the odd one out?

2. Which word in brackets is most opposite in meaning to the word in capitals?

   REVERENT (candid, lucid, cheeky, content, culpable)

3. Identify two words (one from each set of brackets) that have a connection (analogy) with the words in capitals and relate to them in the same way.

   COCHLEA (shell, ear, brain)

   CEREBELLUM (heart, nose, brain)

4. Which number is the odd one out?

   3647 2536 5869 6957 1425 4758

5.

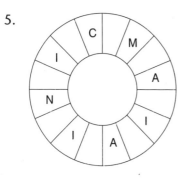

   Read clockwise to find a 16-letter word. Only alternate letters have been shown, and you have to find the starting point.

6. How many lines appear below?

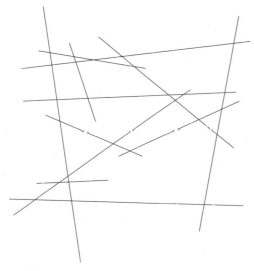

7. 0, 1, 2, 5, 20, 25, ?, ?

   What two numbers should replace the question marks?

8. Which is the odd one out?

exacerbate, alleviate, amplify, escalate, inflate

9.

What number should replace the question mark?

10. The name of which creature can be placed on the bottom row to complete seven three-letter words reading downwards?

D A S A M Y W

U R A G A O A

*   *   *   *   *   *   *

11.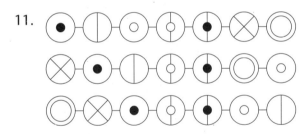

What comes next?

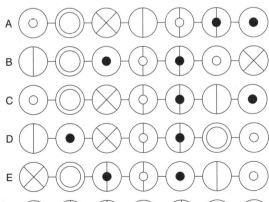

12.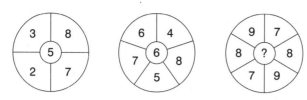

What number should replace the question mark?

13.
	N	E
A	M	T
M		I

Start at one of the four corner letters and spiral clockwise round the perimeter, finishing at the centre letter to spell out a nine-letter word. You must provide the missing letters.

14. In eight years time the combined age of me and my two sons will be 124. What will it be in five years time?

15. Which two words are closest in meaning?

old, stiff, ripe, pure, uniform, mellow

16.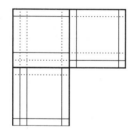

Which is the missing tile?

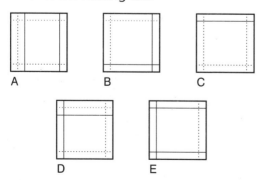

A   B   C

D   E

17. abyss is to chasm as fissure is to: crevice, recess, gorge, canyon, opening

18. Jack is twice as old as Jill, but in five years time he will only be one and a half times as old. How old are Jack and Jill now?

19. Change one letter only in each of the words below to produce a familiar phrase:

    HOME SO LINE

20. ?

    Draw the missing figure in the above sequence.

21. 1000, 865, ?, 595, 460, 325

    What number should replace the question mark?

22.

    Which shield below has most in common with the shield above?

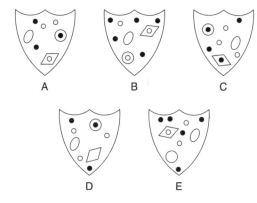

23. Identify two words that sound alike, but are spelled differently, which mean:

    potency
    small insect

24.

14	26	28
91	18	89
57	177	22
189	16	7

Multiply the lowest even number in the grid by the highest odd number.

25. What is the meaning of laconic?

dull, uninspiring
tearful
using few words
emotionally unstable
sarcastic

26.

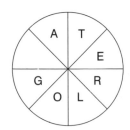

Work clockwise round each circle to spell out two eight-letter words that are synonymous. You have to find the starting points and provide the missing letters.

27. 17, 4, 29, 13, 41, 22, 53, 31, ?

What number should replace the question mark?

28.

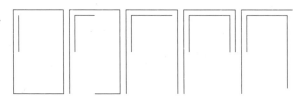

What comes next?

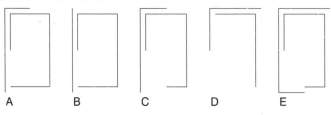

A   B   C   D   E

29.

	T	I
E		M
T	N	O

Spiral clockwise round the perimeter and finish at the centre square to spell out a nine-letter word. You must find the starting point and provide the missing letters.

30.

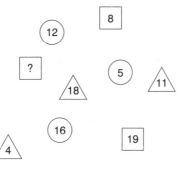

What number should replace the question mark?

31.

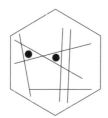

To which hexagon below can a dot be added so that *both* dots then meet the same conditions as the two dots in the hexagon above?

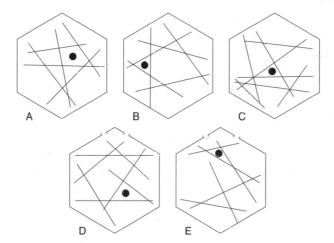

32.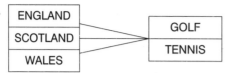

Three teams, from England, Scotland and Wales, are competing for two trophies, one for golf and one for tennis. How many different outcomes of the two competitions exist?

6, 8, 9 or 12?

33. Which is the odd one out?

statement, fluster, retirement, restful, testament

34. Switch A turns lights 1 and 2 on/off or off/on
Switch B turns lights 2 and 4 on/off or off/on
Switch C turns lights 1 and 3 on/off or off/on
Switch D turns lights 3 and 4 on/off or off/on

 = ON

= OFF

Switches B, D, A and C are thrown in turn with the result that Figure 1 turns into Figure 2. Which switch does not work at all?

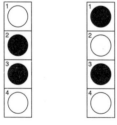

Figure 1   Figure 2

35.

5	7	4	3	1
1	2	2	6	5
6	6	5	?	
1	2			

What number should replace the question mark?

36.

What comes next?

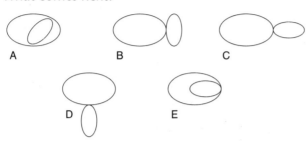

37. Find two words (7, 4) in this diagram. Letters are traced across the circle by chords. If the next letter is four letters or less away, it will be found by tracing around the circumference. Clue: may be difficult to swim over.

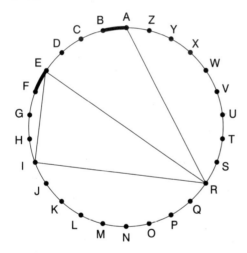

38.

A	B	C	D	E	
F	G	H	I	J	
K	L	M	N	O	
P	Q	R	S	T	
U	V	W	X	Y	Z

What letter is immediately to the left of the letter that is immediately below the letter two to the left of the letter I?

39. Which number is the odd one out?

    3861 8712 5247 4356 1485 3645

40.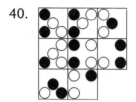

    Which is the missing tile?

    A   B   C   D   E   F   G   H

Questions

1.

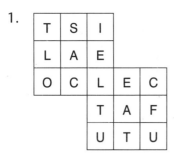

Each square contains the letters of a nine-letter word. Find the two words that are similar in meaning.

2. 1, 3, 4, 7, 11, 18, 29, ?

What number should replace the question mark?

3. Which four bits can be joined together to form two words that have opposite meanings?

ant, ert, uce, ire, ill, and, red, tic, exp

4.

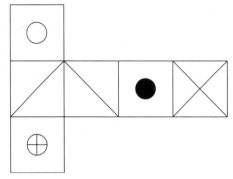

When the above is folded to form a cube, which is the only one of the following that *can* be produced?

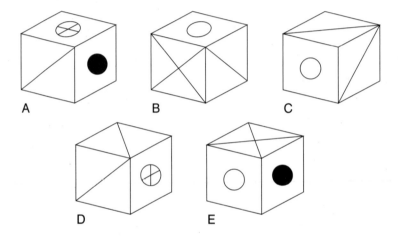

5. blanch is to boil as sauté is to: simmer, fry, soak, roast, garnish

6. In a game of eight players lasting for 70 minutes, six substitutes alternate with each player. This means that all players, including the substitutes, are on the pitch for the same length of time. For how long?

7. If 2 = H are BTO is two heads are better than one, what is the meaning of 2 = S to ES?

8. Which three of the four pieces below can be fitted together to form a perfect square?

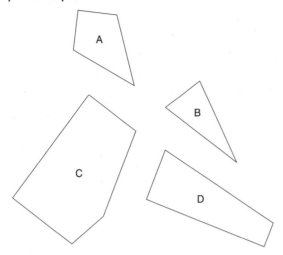

9. Which is the odd one out?

   parabolic, lancet, abutment, trefoil, ogee

10.

8	3	4
9	4	6
12	2	?

   Look at lines both across and down and work out which number should replace the question mark.

11.

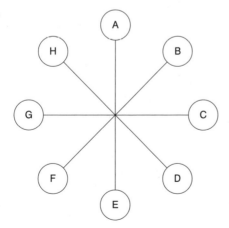

   What letter is directly opposite the letter two places anticlockwise away from the letter directly opposite the letter H?

12.

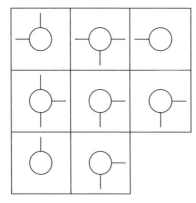

Which is the missing tile?

A

B

C

D

E

13. Change one letter only in each of the words below to produce a familiar phrase:

SO LID ON WANT

14. Insert the numbers 1–5 in the circles so that for any particular circle the sum of the numbers in the circles connected directly to it equals the value corresponding to the number in that circle as given in the list.

Example: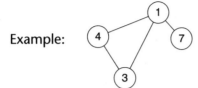

1 = 14 (4 + 3 + 7)
3 = 5 (4 + 1)
4 = 4 (1 + 3)
7 = 1

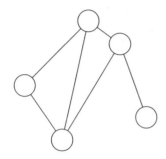

1 = 4
2 = 12
3 = 7
4 = 8
5 = 9

15.

	A	
O	C	I
N	A	P

Start at one of the four corner letters and spiral clockwise round the perimeter, finishing at the centre letter to spell out a nine-letter word. You must provide the missing letters.

16.

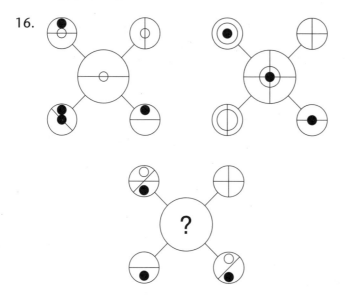

Which circle should replace the question mark?

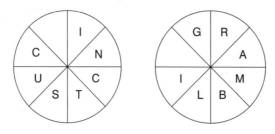

17.

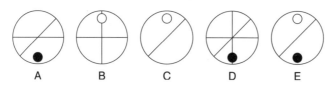

Find two eight-letter words reading clockwise in each circle. The words are antonyms. You have to find the starting point of each word, and provide the missing letter.

18. Which of the following is not an anagram of a type of building?

delta arch
raiment
cleats
the Arctic
a blowgun

19. If five men can build a house in 16 days, how long will it take just two men to build the same house, assuming all men work at the same rate?

20.

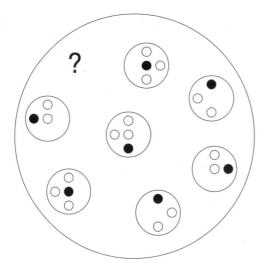

Which circle should replace the question mark?

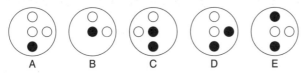

21.

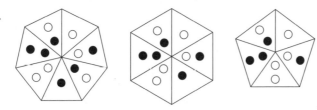

What comes next?

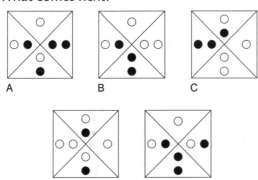

22. Change one letter only in each word to produce a familiar phrase:

    cone do line

23. IQS: LNV
    JRM: ?

    LOP, MOP, LIP, MOW or KIP?

24. 742 (8710) 138
    395 (12167) 972
    819 (?) 356

    What number should replace the question mark?

25. FAIRER BEETLE is an anagram of which two words that are similar in meaning?

26.

    Which hexagon below has most in common with the hexagon above?

A   B   C

D   E

27. Identify two words that sound alike but are spelled differently, which mean:

    regrets
    artifice

28. Simplify:

$$\frac{27}{74} \div \frac{9}{37} \times \frac{6}{17}$$

    to the lowest fraction.

29.

A	B	C	D	E
F	G	H	I	J
K	L	M	N	O
P	Q	R	S	T
U	V	W	X	Y	Z

What letter is two letters to the right of the letter two letters above the letter four letters to the left of the letter Z?

30.

Draw the missing figure in the above sequence.

31.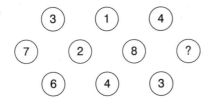

What number should replace the question mark?

32. night long boat house ?

What comes next?

calm, hold, panic, wind, post

33. rifle is to firearm as cutlass is to: blade, sword, weapon, steel, sever

34.

6	7	9	16
4	3	2	4
6	11	5	32
18	10	13	?

What number should replace the question mark?

35.

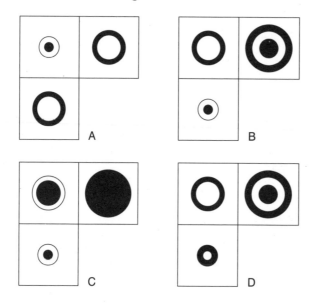

Which is the missing section?

36. 7 4 2 6 3 5 8 1 9

What is the difference between the average of the numbers above and the second lowest even number?

37. How much does a bag of flour weigh if it weighs 1 kilogram plus the weight of half the bag of flour?

38. Fill in the missing letters to find two types of tree:

    *U*A*Y****

    *A*D*L*O**

39.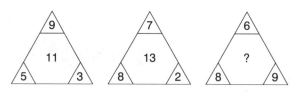

    What number should replace the question mark?

40.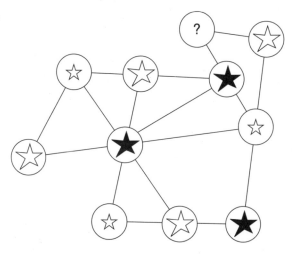

    Which is missing?

    A   B   C

Questions

1.

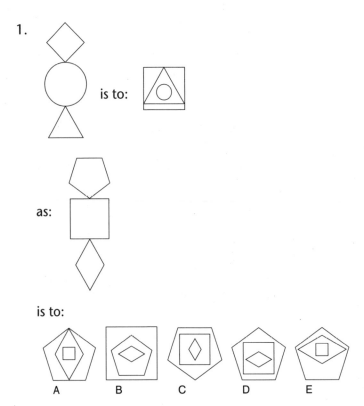

2. Which is the odd one out?

   banner, staff, pennant, streamer, oriflamme

3. Peter, Paul and Mary share out a certain sum of money between them. Peter gets $^2/_5$, Paul gets 0.55 and Mary gets £45.00. How much is the original sum of money?

4.

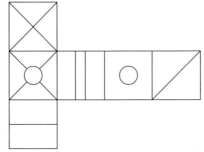

When the above is folded to form a cube, which is the only one of the following that *can* be produced?

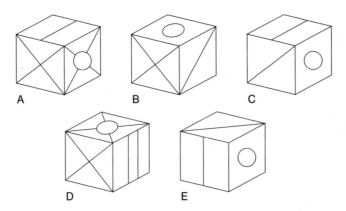

5. Which word in brackets is closest in meaning to the word in capitals?

   INTRINSIC (precursory, interfering, obstinate, elemental, fascinating)

6. Place a four-letter word inside the brackets that will complete a word or phrase when tacked onto the word on the left, and will form another word or phrase when placed in front of the word on the right.

   HEAD (****) LASS

7.

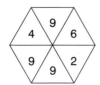

What number should replace the question mark?

8.

1S 1E	2S 1E	2W 1S
1S 1E	1E 1N	1W 1N
1N 2E	T	2N 2W

Find the starting point and visit every square once each to finish at the treasure marked T. 1N 2W means 1 North, 2 West.

9.

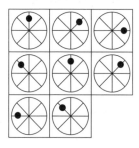

Which is the missing tile?

A   B   C   D   E

10.

20	19	18	17	16
31	28	?	22	19
26	21	16	?	6
26	22	18	14	?

Which is the missing section?

11. Which two words are most opposite in meaning?

    lucrative, proficient, decorous, unskilled, unusual, industrious

12. Identify two words (one from each set of brackets) that have a connection (analogy) with the words in capitals and relate to them in the same way.

    EMBARK (sail, venture, develop)

    INAUGURATE (speech, invent, introduce)

13. Which number is the odd one out?

    571219

    461016

    831114

    461016

    971613

    781523

14. The following clue leads to which pair of rhyming words?

    yank yarn

15.

    What comes next in the above sequence?

    A   B   C   D   E

16. 100, 97.25, 91.75, 83.5, ?

    What number should replace the question mark?

17. dentiform is to tooth as dendriform is to: triangle, tree, doughnut, arch, foot

18. The average of three numbers is 48. The average of two of these numbers is 56. What is the third number?

19. Arrange the three-letter bits below into the correct order to spell out a familiar saying:

    nwo ion der tha eak rds lou ssp act

20. How many different sized circles appear below?

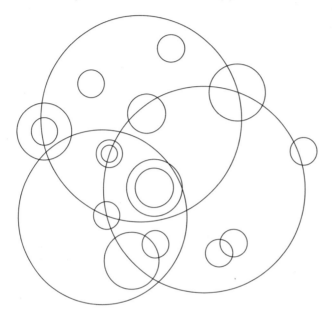

21. What is the longest word in the English language that can be produced from the set of letters below? Letters may only be used once in the word produced.

    MEOIALJTBG

22. The letters below represent a phrase where the initial letters of each word and the spaces have been removed. What is the phrase?

    USHHEOATUT

23.

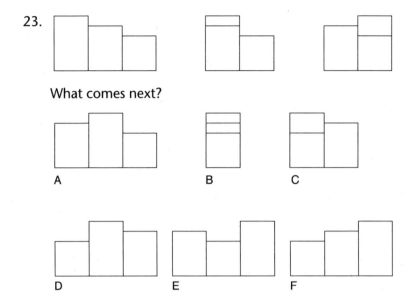

What comes next?

A   B   C

D   E   F

24. 71, 81, 74, 77, 77, 73, 80, 69, ?

What number should replace the question mark?

25. Place a word in the bracket that forms a new word or phrase when tacked onto the word on the left, and another word or phrase when placed in front of the word on the right.

home (   ) fast

26.

5	2		
		9	1
3			9
	8	1	

Insert the remaining numbers below into the grid so that each line across and down totals 21.

6 6 6
5 5 8
7 3

27.

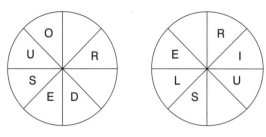

Find the starting point and work anticlockwise round each circle to find two types of creature, each eight letters long. You have to provide the missing letters.

28.

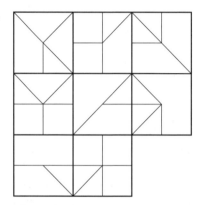

Which is the missing tile?

A

B

C

D

E

F

29.

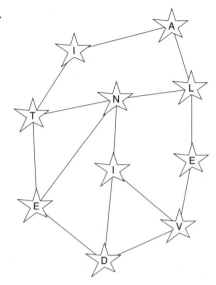

Move from star to star along connecting lines to spell out a 10-letter word. All letters are used once each only.

30.

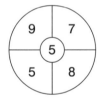 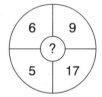

What number should replace the question mark?

31.

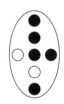

Which is missing?

A   B   C   D   E

32.

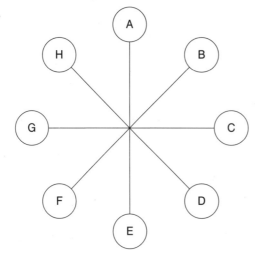

What letter is directly opposite the letter that is two letters away clockwise from the letter that is directly opposite the letter that is three letters away anti-clockwise from the letter E?

33. In 13 years time the combined ages of my three brothers will be 94. What will it be in nine years time?

34.

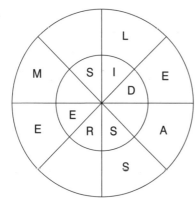

Find two words, one reading clockwise round the outer circle, and one reading anticlockwise round the inner circle, which are opposite in meaning. You must provide the missing letters.

35.

	7		8		12
2	21	8	35	8	?	?
	4		11		7

What numbers should replace the question marks?

36.

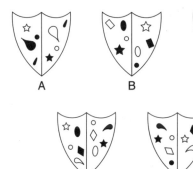

Which shield below has most in common with the shield above?

A   B   C

D   E

37.   Switch A turns lights 1 and 2 on/off or off/on
      Switch B turns lights 2 and 4 on/off or off/on
      Switch C turns lights 1 and 3 on/off or off/on
      Switch D turns lights 3 and 4 on/off or off/on

   = ON

⭘   = OFF

Switches C, A, D and B are thrown in turn with the result that Figure 1 turns into Figure 2. Which switch does not work at all?

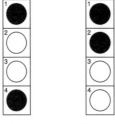

Figure 1   Figure 2

38.

A	P	B		
E	T	L		
A	A	L	S	S
		T	E	T
		A	S	E

Each square contains the letters of a nine-letter word. Find the two nine-letter words that are antonyms.

39.

5	7	4	9	8	2	7
3	8	6	4	7	5	9
9	6	1	4	5	8	?

What number should replace the question mark?

40.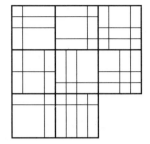

Which is the missing tile?

A   B   C   D   E

Test 8

Questions

1. 0, 1, 3, 6, 7, 9, 12, 13, 15, 18, ?, ?, ?

   What numbers should replace the question marks?

2. Find two words that differ only by the omission of a single letter (for example, place/pace), in answer to the following clue:

   bowl-shaped cavity/provide food

3.

43	6	16	12	24
2	22	1	4	9
46	30	48	5	13
38	8	36	7	3
11	20	14	10	15

   What number in the grid is three places away from itself less two, two places away from itself divided by two, three places away from itself less five and three places away from itself multiplied by three?

4.

A	C	F
E	?	J
J	L	?

   Which is the missing section?

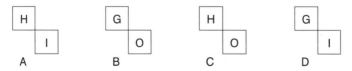

   A   B   C   D

5.

To which of the squares below can a dot be added so that the dot then meets the same conditions as the dot in the square above?

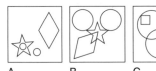

A   B   C   D   E

6. Complete the following to create a palindromic phrase, ie one that reads the same forwards and backwards, such as Madam I'm Adam.

*U**L* ***P **

Clue: scholarly errors!

7. 8 3   6 4   4 5   ? ?
   9 6   6 5   3 4   ? ?

What numbers should replace the question marks?

8.

 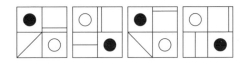

Draw the missing figure in the above sequence.

9. Which is the odd one out?

sow, bull, buck, boar, stallion

10. The ages of five family members total 107 between them.

The ages of Margaret and Stuart total 29 between them.
The ages of Stuart and Jeffrey total 44 between them.
The ages of Jeffrey and Brian total 57 between them.
The ages of Brian and Philip total 46 between them.

How old is each family member?

11. IVY CITRATE is an anagram of which two 10-letter words in the English language?

12.

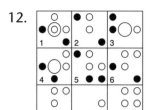

Looking at lines across and down, if the first two tiles are combined to produce the third tile, with the exception that like symbols are cancelled out, which of the above tiles is incorrect, and with which of the tiles below should it be replaced?

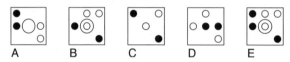

A   B   C   D   E

13. Which two words are most opposite in meaning?

watertight, humid, tractable, opulent, portentous, tenuous

14.

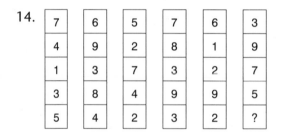

7	6	5	7	6	3
4	9	2	8	1	9
1	3	7	3	2	7
3	8	4	9	9	5
5	4	2	3	2	?

What number should replace the question mark?

15. Add three consecutive letters of the alphabet to the group of letters below, without splitting the consecutive letters of the alphabet, to form another word.

GERE

16.

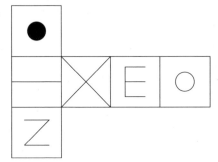

When the above is folded to form a cube, which is the only one of the following that *can* be produced?

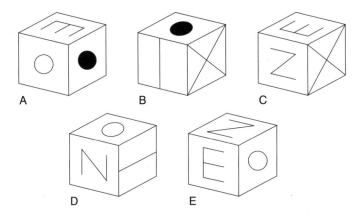

17. closed is to shut as open is to: obscure, visible, field, overt, wide

18. Harry is one and a third as old as Larry and Larry is one and a third as old as Carrie. Together their ages total 74. How old are Larry, Harry and Carrie?

19. Which two words are closest in meaning?

salubrious, healthy, identical, conspicuous, devout, bleak

20.   is to:

as:

is to:

A⁻   B   C

D   E   F

21.

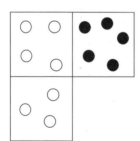

Which is the missing tile?

A   B   C

D   E

22. Find two words, both reading clockwise round each circle. You must find the starting point of each word and provide the missing letters. The two words form a phrase.

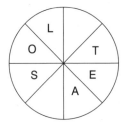 

23. Switch A turns lights 1 and 2 on/off or off/on
    Switch B turns lights 2 and 4 on/off or off/on
    Switch C turns lights 1 and 3 on/off or off/on
    Switch D turns lights 3 and 4 on/off or off/on

     = ON

     = OFF

    Switches A, C, D and B are thrown in turn with the result that Figure 1 turns into Figure 2. Which switch does not work at all?

   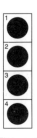

Figure 1   Figure 2

24. 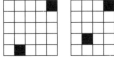 ?

    Which is missing?

A   B   C   D   E

25. The letters below represent a phrase where the initial letters of each word and the spaces have been removed. What is the phrase?

    INEFORK

26.

23	24	41
57	92	91
18	16	28
56	21	19

    Multiply the highest odd number in the grid by the lowest even number.

27. Only one group of five letters below can be rearranged to spell out a five-letter word in the English language. Identify the word.

    LEVUR

    TNIEC

    HEOLC

    ANOIP

    IRNAL

28. 1, 2.25, 3.75, 5.5, 7.5, 9.75, ?

    What number should replace the question mark?

29. Place a word in the bracket that forms a new word or phrase when tacked onto the word on the left, and another word or phrase when placed in front of the word on the right.

    second (   ) some

30.

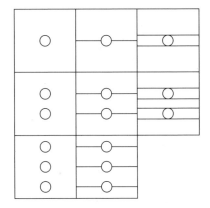

Which is the missing tile?

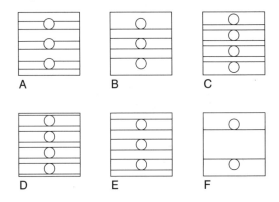

31. How many minutes is it before midnight if 32 minutes ago it was three times as many minutes past 22.00?

32. boater, nail, about, ruin, alibi, ?

Which word below comes next in the above sequence?

stray, tiara, treat, suit, trail

33.

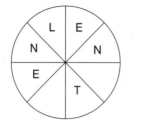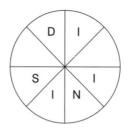

Work clockwise round the circles to spell out two eight-letter words that are antonyms. Each word commences in a different circle, and you must find the starting point of each. Every letter is used once each and all letters are consecutive.

34. 1, 31, 59, 85, 109, ?

What number should replace the question mark?

35.

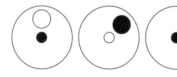

Draw the missing figure in the above sequence.

36.

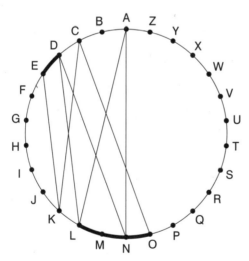

Find two words (4, 6) in this diagram. Letters are traced across the circle by chords. If the next letter is four letters or less away, it will be found by tracing around the circumference. Clue: no coastline

37.

E	L	I
	F	E
	I	D

Start at one of the four corner letters and spiral clockwise round the perimeter, finishing at the centre letter to spell out a nine-letter word. You must provide the missing letters.

38.   What is $\dfrac{5}{9}$ divided by $\dfrac{15}{18}$?

39.   Three coins are tossed in the air and two of the coins land with heads face upwards. What are the chances on the next toss of the coins that at least two of the coins will land with heads face upwards again?

40.

Which shield below has most in common with the shield above?

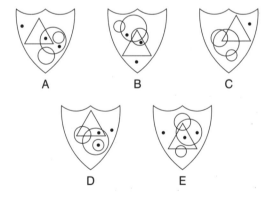

Questions

1.

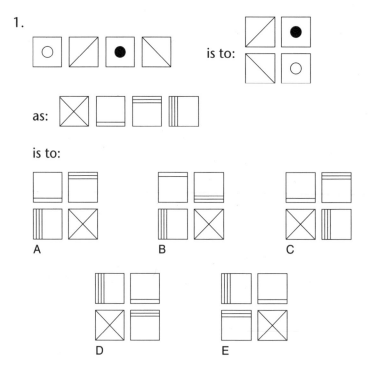

2. VEILED HARE is an anagram of which two words that are opposite in meaning?

3. Add one letter, not necessarily the same letter, to the beginning, middle or end of the words below to find five new words all on the same theme.

   back live fan can pin

4.

1	3	5	7
4	8	?	16
7	?	19	25
10	18	?	34

Which is the missing section?

	12
13	
	26

A

	14
14	
	24

B

	13
12	
	26

C

	13
14	
	24

D

5. A B C D E F G H

Which letter is two to the left of the letter that is four to the right of the letter immediately to the right of the letter A?

6. Which is the odd one out?

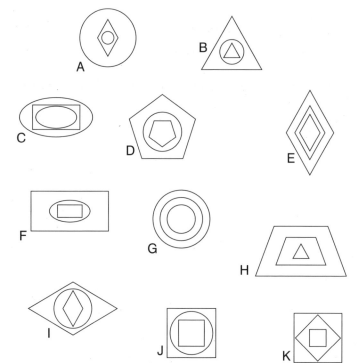

7.

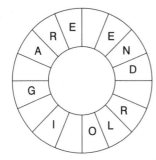

Find a familiar phrase (6, 6, 4) reading clockwise. You have to find the starting point and provide the missing letters.

8.

What number should replace the question mark?

9. eastern, reality, titanic, ?

Which of the words below comes next?

natural, omnibus, include, devious or shingle

10. Which three of the pieces below, when fitted together, will form a perfect square?

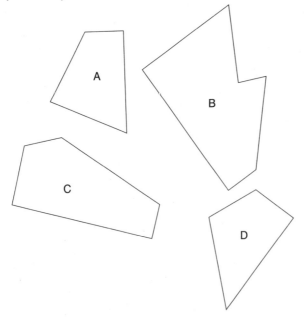

11. RASCAL MARE is an anagram of which two words that are similar in meaning?

12. gallery is to balcony as stalls is to: proscenium, stage, audience, footlights, pit

13. 3182596 is to 65283

    and 6742835 is to 53476

    therefore 7496258 is to ?

14. A, C, F, J, O, ?

    What letter comes next?

15.

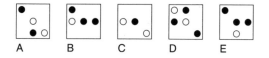

    Looking at lines across and down, if the first two tiles are combined to produce the third tile, with the exception that like symbols are cancelled out, which of the above tiles is incorrect, and with which of the tiles below should it be replaced?

    A   B   C   D   E

16. 0, 27, 54, ?, 108, 135

    What number should replace the question mark?

17. Which is the odd one out?

    bolero, calypso, waltz, salsa, polka

18.

6	10	14	18
9	13	?	21
12	?	20	24
15	?	23	27

Which section is missing?

19. I met four of my old school friends today. In the morning I first saw Patricia and later bumped into Richie. Then in the afternoon I saw Christabel. Who did I encounter in the evening? Was it Thora, Stella, Thelma or Sally?

20.

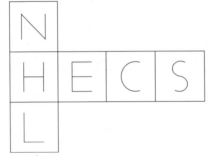

When the above is folded to form a cube, which is the only one of the following that can be produced?

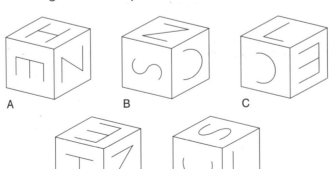

21.

Which shield below has most in common with the shield above?

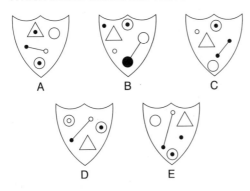

A   B   C

D   E

22.

7	4	5	2
5	1	9	3
2	9	1	6
?	4	3	7

What number should replace the question mark?

23.

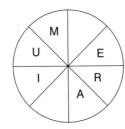
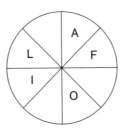

Find the starting point and work clockwise round each circle to find two types of flower, each eight letters long. You have to provide the missing letters.

24.

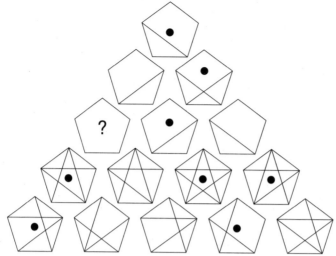

Which is missing?

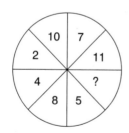

A   B   C   D   E

25. Using all of the letters in the phrase TOUCH VOLCANO PIECE once each only spell out the names of three types of fruit.

26.

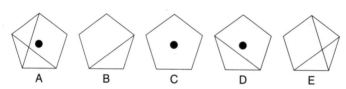

What number should replace the question mark?

27.

Draw the missing figure in the above sequence.

28. ASH FUEL FARM is an anagram of which two words that are opposite in meaning?

29.

171	23	18
17	19	29
78	56	27
28	71	82

Multiply the highest even number in the grid by the lowest odd number.

30. action, effort, worth, ?, ourself

Which of the words below is missing?

cheer, reef, cage, rampart, idea

31.

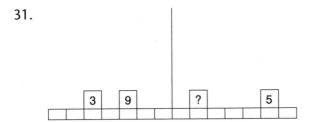

What weight should replace the question mark in order for the scales to balance?

32.

4	9	13	5	86	2	7
82						9
79						24
6						63
35						18
1	6	37	8	49	2	?

What number should replace the question mark?

33.

What comes next?

A　　　　B　　　　C　　　　D　　　　E

34. Place a word in the bracket that forms a new word or phrase when tacked onto the word on the left, and another word or phrase when placed in front of the word on the right.

salt (　　　) fall

35. Which is the odd word out?

orders, murder, derelict, underworld, detonator

36. Stuart and Christine share out a certain sum of money in the ratio 4:5 and Christine ends up with £24.00. How much money was shared in the first place?

37. Referring again to question 36, how much money would have been shared out if the ratio had been 5:4 instead of 4:5?

38.

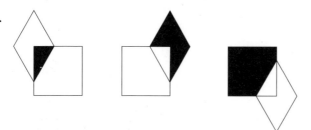

What comes next?

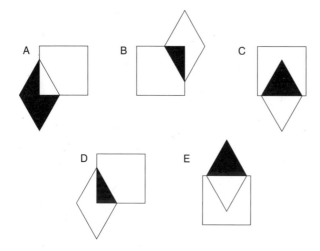

39.

S	I	P	Y
E	A	R	
	O	R	T

Find the starting point and work from letter to adjoining letter horizontally and vertically, but not diagonally, to spell out a 12-letter word. You have to provide the missing letters.

40.

7	9	4	5
13	11	14	9
25	27	20	23
47	45	50	43
?	?	?	?

What numbers should replace the question marks on the bottom row?

1.

5	3
8	12
7	5

4	5
14	6
2	9

7	8
?	13
6	9

What number should replace the question mark?

2. Which word in brackets is most opposite in meaning to the word in capitals?
PALATABLE (sparse, agonising, bland, raw, inferior)

3. 100, 99.5, 98.5, 97, 95, 92.5, 89.5, ?
What number should replace the question mark?

4. Switch A turns lights 1 and 2 on/off or off/on
Switch B turns lights 2 and 4 on/off or off/on
Switch C turns lights 1 and 3 on/off or off/on

○ = ON

● = OFF

Switches B, A and C are thrown in turn with the result that Figure 1 turns into Figure 2. Which switch does not work at all?

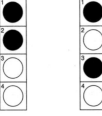

Figure 1   Figure 2

5.

To which shield below can a dot be added so that it meets the same conditions as in the shield above?

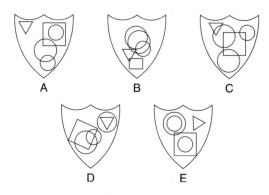

A   B   C

D   E

6. Which is the odd one out?

   diploid, deltoid, dual, binary, twofold

7.

5	10	9	4
7	4	5	8
3	2	5	6
1	8	9	?

What number should replace the question mark?

8. Insert a pair of letters into each bracket so that they finish the word on the left and start the word on the right. The correct letters read down-wards in pairs must spell out an eight-letter word.

   SO (**) LT

   LA (**) ST

   DO (**) AL

   EP (**) ON

9. Which is the odd one out?

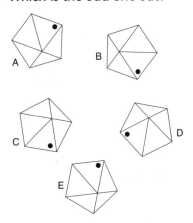

10. Which one of the following is grammatically correct?

The father's rights activist's dog buried its bone in the garden.
The fathers' rights activist's dog buried it's bone in the garden.
The father's rights activist's dog buried it's bone in the garden.
The fathers' rights' activist's dog buried its bone in the garden.
The fathers' rights activists' dog buried it's bone in the garden.
The fathers' rights activist's dog buried its bone in the garden.
The father's rights activists' dog buried its bone in the garden.

11. Which number is the odd one out?

6394, 9416, 5278, 6231, 9614, 6132, 7895, 5872, 7598

12.

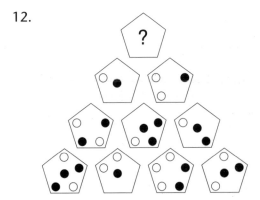

Which pentagon should replace the question mark?

13. Which word in brackets is closest in meaning to the word in capitals?

    SPARTAN (scarce, austere, erratic, limited, fierce)

14. Only one set of letters below can be rearranged into a six-letter word in the English language. Find the word.

    HURLPO

    KCIENA

    WINCAL

    EJBATC

    XELPOD

    NWIOLM

15. 7964325 is to 6975234

    and 5822139 is to 2859312

    therefore 7469851 is to ?

16.

    Which shield below has most in common with the shield above?

    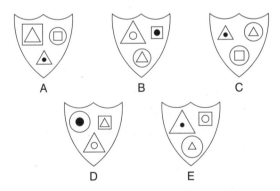

17. caster is to chair as rowel is to: wheel, spur, bicycle, pulley, gyroscope

18. Insert the numbers 1–6 in the circles so that for any particular circle the sum of the numbers in the circles connected directly to it equals the value corresponding to the numbers in that circle as given in the list.

Example: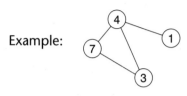

1 = 4
3 = 11 (4 + 7)
4 = 11 (1 + 3 + 7)
7 = 7 (4 + 3)

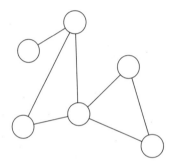

1 = 8
2 = 4
3 = 6
4 = 13
5 = 14
6 = 9

19. What four-letter word can be placed in the bracket to form a word when tacked onto the end of blue and another word when placed in front of owed?

BLUE (****) OWED

20.

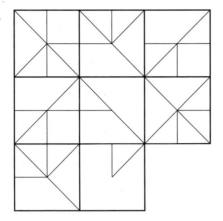

Which is the missing tile?

A   B   C

D   E

21.

Which is the missing square?

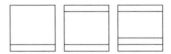

A   B   C   D   E   F

22. Which two words are closest in meaning?
    lonely, haughty, crafty, credulous, careful, arrogant

23. Switch A turns lights 1 and 2 on/off or off/on
    Switch B turns lights 2 and 4 on/off or off/on
    Switch C turns lights 1 and 3 on/off or off/on
    Switch D turns lights 3 and 4 on/off or off/on

 = ON

○ = OFF

Switches D, B, C and A are thrown in turn with the result that Figure 1 turns into Figure 2. Which switch does not work at all?

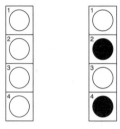

Figure 1   Figure 2

24. Using all of the letters in the phrase A CATASTROPHIC PROTON only once each spell out the names of three types of vegetable.

25.

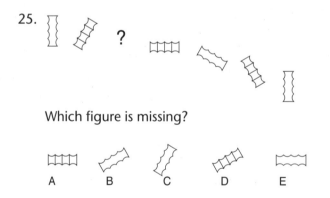

Which figure is missing?

A   B   C   D   E

26. Which two words are most opposite in meaning?

validation, revival, sarcasm, extinction, rebellion, fissure

27.

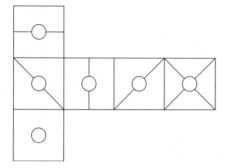

When the above is folded to form a cube, which is the only one of the following that *can* be produced?

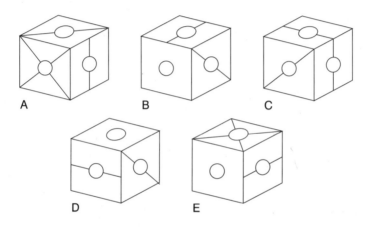

28. Which word in brackets is most opposite in meaning to the word in capitals?

SENSIBLE (unaware, subordinate, irrational, outlandish, irreverent)

29. 9, 16, 13, 13, 17, 10, 21, 7, ?

What number should replace the question mark?

30. dirty, berry, hint, knot

Which one word below shares a common feature with all four words above?

part, cost, near, find, open

31. AFFIRM DEMON is an anagram of which phrase (5, 2, 4)? Clue: inclination.

32.

Which square below has most in common with the square above?

A   B   C

D   E

33. 70   91   120
     14   13   24
      5   7   ?

What number should replace the question mark?

34. A B C D E F G H

What letter is two letters to the right of the letter immediately to the left of the letter four letters to the right of the letter two letters to the left of the letter E?

35. POLLUTE SPICE is an anagram of which phrase (4, 2, 6)? Clue: demolish.

36.

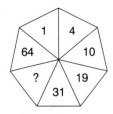

What number should replace the question mark?

37.

    To which hexagon below can a dot be added so that it then meets the same conditions as in the hexagon above?

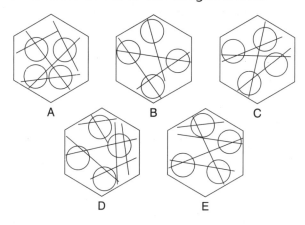

    A   B   C

    D   E

38. A greengrocer received a boxful of tomatoes and on opening the box found that several had gone bad. He then counted them up so that he could make a formal complaint and found that 68 were mouldy, which was 16 per cent of the total contents of the box. How many tomatoes were in the box?

39. EMPTY (PRISM) VIRUS

    DEPTH (*****) DUALS

    What word is coded to appear in the second bracket?

40.

    What number should replace the question mark?

Questions

1.

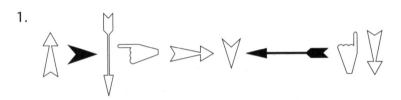

Which two arrows come next?

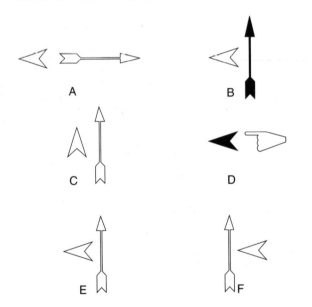

2. PIANIST RULES is an anagram of which two words that are opposite in meaning?

3. Work from letter to adjacent letter, horizontally, vertically or diagonally to spell out a 12-letter word. You must find the starting point and provide the missing letters.

I	T	S	*
A	L	O	O
N	C	O	*

4. How many minutes is it before 12 noon if 16 minutes ago it was three times as many minutes after 9 am?

5.

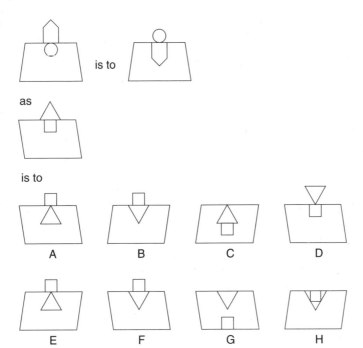

6. Which is the odd one out?

   vixen, vulpine, reynard, lupine, brush

7. Which word can be placed in the brackets that has the same meaning as the words either side of the brackets?

   ARMADA (– – – – –) SWIFT

8. Insert the correct numbers to replace the question marks.

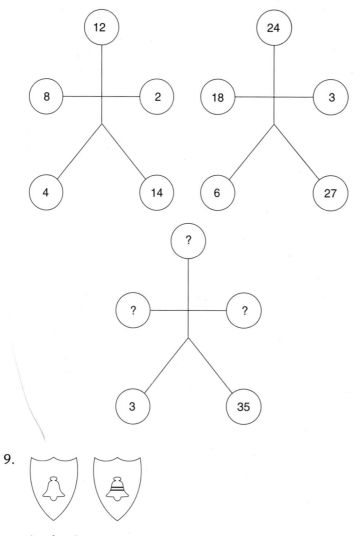

9.

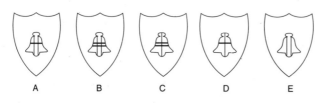

Which is the missing shield?

10. Beaufort is to wind as Munsell is to:

    music, colour, minerals, weight, intelligence

11. Solve the cryptic clue. The answer is a nine-letter word anagram within the clue:

    wise bands deteriorate into lasciviousnes

12. 64521 is to 41256 as 38297 is to:

    a. 89732;   b. 29873;

    c. 92837;   d. 87923;

    e. 87932.

13. How many lines appear below?

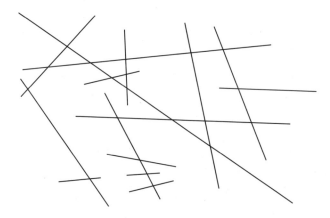

14. Complete the two eight-letter words that are synonyms, one reading clockwise and the other anticlockwise. In each word, you must provide the missing letters and find the starting points.

 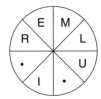

15. Find a word that when tacked onto the end of the first word produces another word or phrase and when placed in front of the second word produces another word or phrase.

    BONE (_ _ _ _ _) TOWN

16. What number comes next in this sequence?

    1, 3, 11, 47, ?

17.

Which is the missing segment?

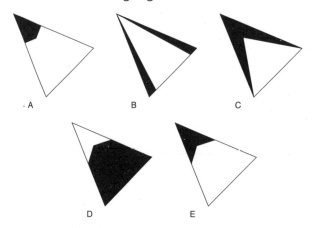

18. Change one letter only in each word to produce a familiar phrase. go hit us

19. What number comes next in this sequence?

    100, 97.25, 91.75, 83.5, ?

20. Which is the odd one out?

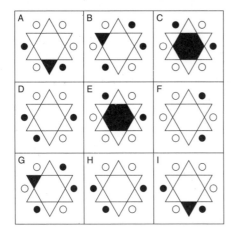

21. Which of the following is not a colour or colour shade?

    such tent   cap riot   red navel   cats lie   for fans

22.

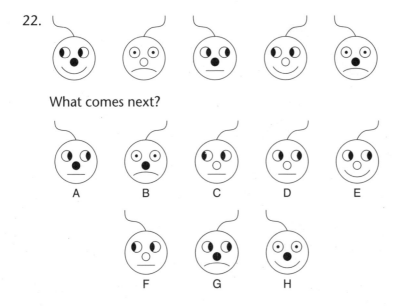

What comes next?

23. Find a magic number square in the grid where all lines, ie, horizontal, vertical and corner to corner, add up to the same total.

25	21	19	20	35	45
22	20	24	5	10	30
18	23	26	40	25	15
7	15	25	9	13	11
8	17	10	15	10	14
16	12	14	16	12	17
3	13	18	11	9	8

24. Which is the odd one out?

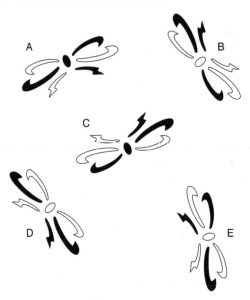

25. Which is the odd one out?

frisk, gambol, frolic, romp, lope

26. Complete the words so that the last two letters of the first word are the first two letters of the second word etc. The last two letters of the fourth word must also be the first two letters of the first word to complete the circle.

CO   **SS**   **AP**   **RI**

27. A train travelling at a speed of 50 mph enters a tunnel that is 1.75 miles long. The length of the train is 3/8 miles. How long does it take for all the train to pass through the tunnel, from the moment the front enters to the moment the rear emerges?

28. How many lines appear below?

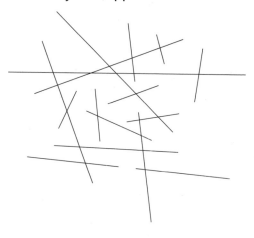

29. dormitory is to sleep as refectory is to:

    study, eat, meet, pray, speak

30. SUNDAY   MONDAY   TUESDAY   WEDNESDAY
    THURSDAY   FRIDAY   SATURDAY

    Which day comes three days before the day that comes two days after the day that comes two days after the day that comes three days before Wednesday?

31. What numbers should replace the question marks?

3	8	2	9	1
5	7	6	4	5
8	5	8	6	7
1	9	2	8	3
5	4	6	7	5
?	?	?	?	?

32. Which is the odd one out?

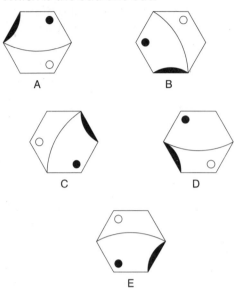

33. Insert the same three letters into the blank spaces to find two words that are opposite in meaning.

    – – –   F A N E
    – – –   P E R

34. Only one of the sets of five letters below can be rearranged to spell out a five-letter English word. Find the word.

    JUCBI   NEACH   METAP   TPHED   MUDOP   ABUMG   ERVIC

35. What number should replace the question mark?

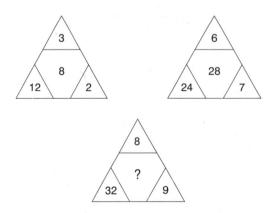

36. Which is the odd one out?

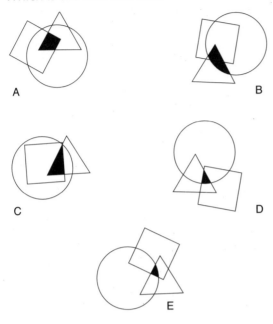

A

B

C

D

E

37. What is the meaning of adumbrate?

    a. come forward;

    b. to obscure;

    c. flattery;

    d. appeal to;

    e. speak off the cuff.

38. Insert the letters into the grid to form two words that together form a phrase.

    LLY   COT   EVA   TEN   MR

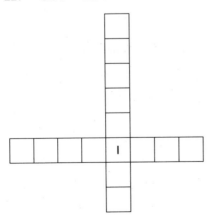

39. Insert the numbers into the circles so that, for any particular circle, the sum of the numbers in the circles connected to it equals the value corresponding to that circled number in the list.

For example:

1 = 14 (4 + 7 + 3)

4 = 8 (7 + 1)

7 = 5 (4 + 1)

3 = 1

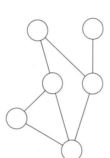

1 = 15

2 = 5

3 = 9

4 = 10

5 = 6

6 = 5

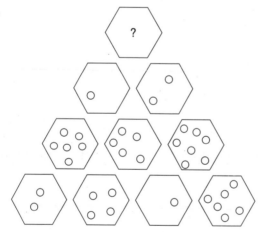

40.

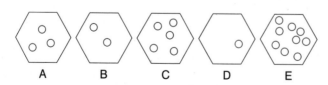

Which hexagon should replace the question mark?

A   B   C   D   E

Questions

1.

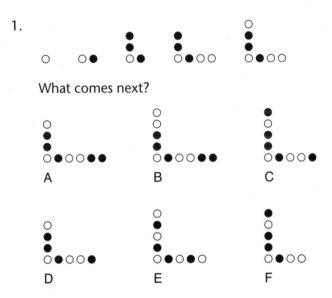

What comes next?

2. MEAN ACTORS is an anagram of which two words that are similar in meaning?

3. Start at one of the corner squares and spiral clockwise around the perimeter to spell out a nine-letter word, finishing at the centre square. You have to provide the missing letters.

A	S	S
*	T	T
*	A	E

4. A man jogs at 6 mph over a certain journey and walks back over the same journey at 3 mph. What is his average speed for the journey?

5.

The contents of which shield below are most like the contents of the shield above?

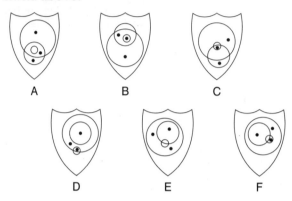

A   B   C

D   E   F

6. Which word can be placed in the brackets that has the same meaning as the definitions either side of the brackets?

IMPEDE (– – – – – –) LARGE BASKET

7. If a car had increased its average speed for a 210-mile journey by 5 mph, the journey would have been completed in one hour less. What was the original speed of the car for the journey?

8.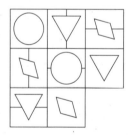

Which is the missing square?

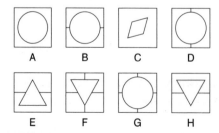

A   B   C   D

E   F   G   H

9. Which is the odd one out?

   mollify, mitigate, indurate, macerate, temper

10. Solve the cryptic clue. The answer is a 13-letter word anagram within the clue:

    reword a keen phrase as in classic theatrical tradition

11. Which word below is in the wrong column?

    sinistral   recto
    southpaw   dextral
    larboard   verso
                           starboard

12. What number should replace the question mark?

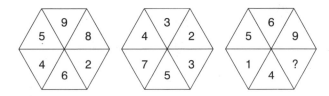

13.

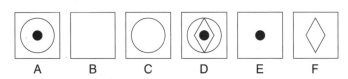

What comes next?

    A   B   C   D   E   F

14. passé is to outmoded as obsolete is to:stale, superseded, antediluvian, vintage, timeworn

15. Find the starting point and work from letter to letter horizontally, vertically or diagonally to spell out a 17-letter phrase.

    E   S   N
    K   L   O
    I   R   I   K   E
              E   L   F
              H   T   A

16. At 12 noon my watch was correct. However, it then started to lose 18 minutes per hour. Four hours ago it stopped completely and is now showing the time as 15.30. What is the correct time?

17.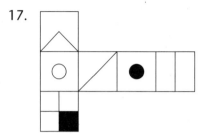

When the above is folded to form a cube, which one of the following can be produced?

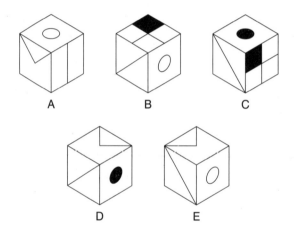

A   B   C

D   E

18. Which of the following is not an anagram of a type of building?

spoil hat   my bases   pet hens   eel clog   admit us

19. What continues the following sequence?

1, 2.65, 4.3, 5.95, 7.6, ?

20.

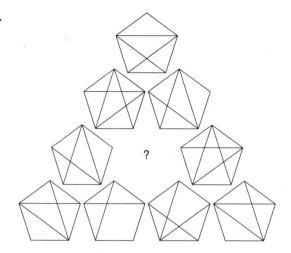

Which is the missing pentagon?

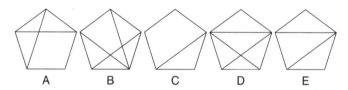

21.

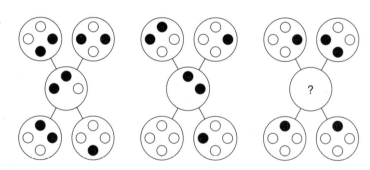

Which circle should replace the question mark?

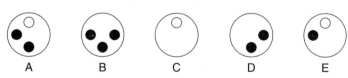

22. Which of these two words are most opposite in meaning?
wizened, witless, plump, lavish, taciturn, feasible

23. Solve the cryptic clue. The answer is a 13-letter word anagram within the clue:

    redraw tennis cartoon with trepidation

24. What number should replace the question mark?

    42   15   14
    56   35   8
    36   ?   4

25.

    What comes next?

        A   B

        C   D

26. Which word in brackets is closest in meaning to the word in capitals?

    FINESSE (cessation, cleverness, showiness, excellence, opening)

27. Find a word that when tacked onto the end of the first word produces another word or phrase and when placed in front of the second word produces another word or phrase.

    FREE (– – – –) APART

28.

What value of weight should be placed on the scales to balance?

29. Which is the odd one out?

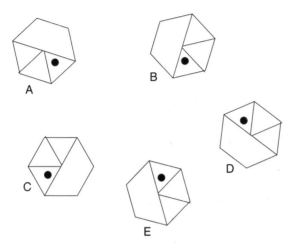

30. Change one letter only in each word to produce a familiar phrase:

dear if bear put

31. What number should replace the question mark?

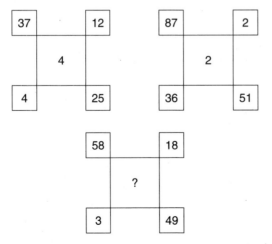

32.

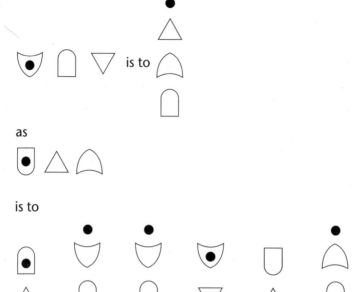

as

is to

| A | B | C | D | E | F |

33. Which is the odd one out?

fedora, sabot, tarboosh, biretta, cloche

34. Place a three-letter word in the brackets that has the same meaning as the definitions either side of the brackets.

a demand for payment (– – –) a brownish-grey colour

35. What number should replace the question mark?

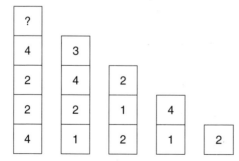

36. Which is the odd one out?

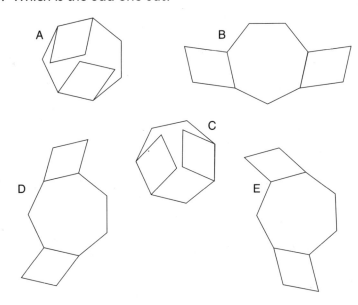

37. palmate is to hand as auriculate is to: nose, face, ear, smell, heel

38. Work from letter to adjacent letter horizontally, vertically and
    diagonally to spell out a 17-letter phrase.

    V   O   D
    E   E   N
    R   B   B   R   A
              A   W   D
              K   C   S

39. What number should replace the question mark?

5	7	4
8	3	6
2	0	1

2	1	2
1	7	1
4	5	6

3	2	4
1	?	3
4	5	3

40.

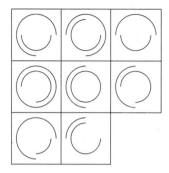

Which is the missing square?

A	B	C	D
E	F	G	H

Questions

1. Place the letters correctly into the quadrants indicated so that two words of opposite meaning are produced, one reading round the inner circle and one round the outer circle. One word will appear clockwise and the other anticlockwise.

NE: READ

SE: YONA

NW: VOTE

SW: BILT

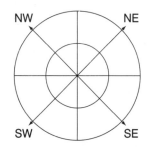

2. Which is the odd one out?

A

B

C

D

3. Solve the cryptic clue. The answer is an 11-letter word anagram within the clue:

   inspect tiny article puzzlingly

4. What number should replace the question mark?

   78214 : 292

   38421 : 459

   69517 : ?

5.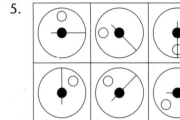

   Which is the missing square?

   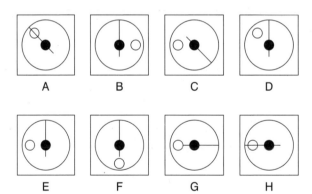

   A   B   C   D

   E   F   G   H

6. emancipate is to slavery as liberate is to: domination, burden, duty, responsibility, captivity

7. Insert two letters into each set of brackets so that they finish the word on the left and start the word on the right. The four pairs of letters inserted when read downards in pairs will spell out an eight-letter word.

    MA (**) AR

    TE (**) ID

    PI (**) RT

    TI (**) AL

8. Midway through his round a golfer hits a magnificent 210-yard drive, which brings his average length per drive for the round up to now from 156 to 162 yards. How far would he have had to hit the drive to bring his average length of drive up from 156 to 165 yards?

9.

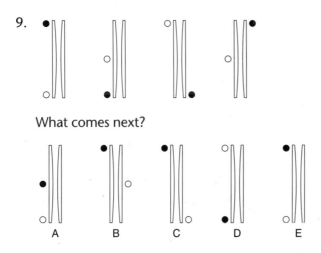

    What comes next?

    A   B   C   D   E

10. Which is the odd one out?

    segment, aggregate, ensemble, compliment, plenitude

11. Which two rhyming words mean smash garden tool?

12. Tom and Harry share a certain sum of money in the ratio 3 : 5. If Harry has £240, how much money is shared?

13.
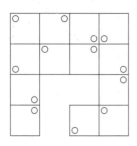

Which is the missing segment?

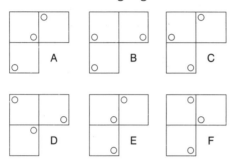

14. Which of the following is not an anagram of a job or profession?

rein gene   lee crock   can chime   mean lass   no treaty

15. What number should replace the question mark?

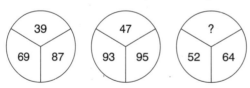

16. Which is the odd one out?

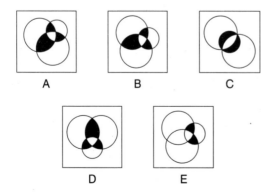

17. Seven synonyms of the keyword TREMENDOUS are listed. Take one letter in turn from each of the seven synonyms to spell out a further synonym of the keyword.

    great, terrific, monstrous, vast, enormous, gigantic, colossal

18. Which set of letters is the odd one out?

    LMNQP   EFGJI   RSTWV   IJKON   OPQTS

19.

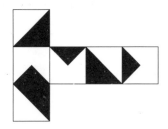

5	4	8	1	7
1	7	3	2	7
9	3	4	6	5
8	9	4	6	8
6	2	4	1	2

5	1	9	8	3
8	2	4	8	1
7	6	1	2	9
7	4	2	6	7
3	7	5	1	9

Find a string of four numbers in the first grid that also appears as a string of four numbers in the same order in the second grid. However, in each grid the string of four numbers may appear reading forwards, backwards, vertically, horizontally or diagonally.

20.

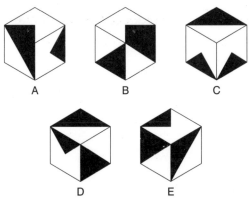

When the above is folded to form a cube, just one of the following can be produced. Which one?

A   B   C

D   E

21. Which is the odd one out?

A

B

C

D

22. Which two words are closest in meaning?

functional, vestigial, rudimentary, proficient, disappointing, savage

23. Find a word that when tacked onto the end of the first word produces another word or phrase and when placed in front of the second word produces another word or phrase.

WELL   OUT

24. What number should replace the question mark?

3   8   6   36
7   4   2   14
6   8   4   48
9   6   2   ?

25. Change one letter only in each word to produce a familiar phrase.

so might say on

26. Which line of figures is the odd one out?

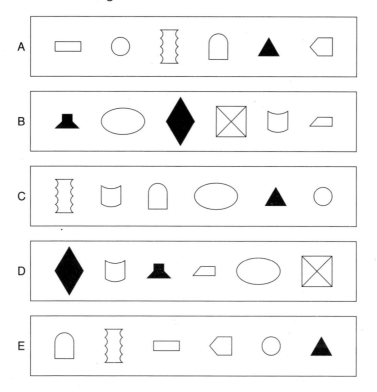

27. What number should replace the question mark?

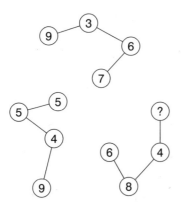

28.

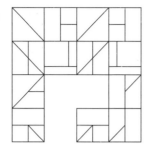

Which is the missing segment?

A   B   C

D   E   F

29. Which word in brackets is most opposite to the word in capitals?

IMPECUNIOUS (accessible, tolerant, affluent, flawed, mortal)

30. Solve the anagram in brackets (12-letter word) to complete the quotation by Alfred North Whitehead.

We think in (agile entries); we live in detail.

31.

Insert the numbers 1–6 inclusive in the circles so that:

the sum of the numbers 4 and 5 and all the numbers in between = 19;

the sum of the numbers 6 and 3 and all the numbers in between = 10;

the sum of the numbers 2 and 1 and all the numbers in between = 11;

the sum of the numbers 4 and 3 and all the numbers in between = 14.

32.

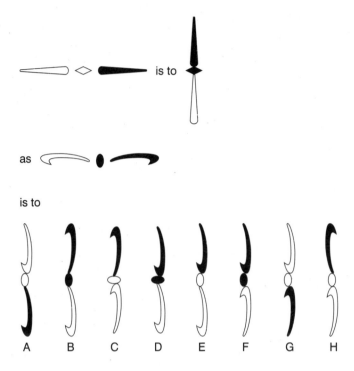

as

is to

A   B   C   D   E   F   G   H

33. Which is the odd one out?

devise, contemplate, contrive, design, concoct

34. Solve the anagrams to find one word that is opposite in meaning to the rest.

rude tie   no rating   dear Len   elite art

35. Which number is the odd one out?

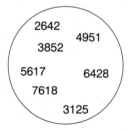

36.

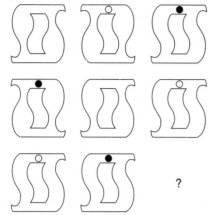

Which figure should replace the question mark?

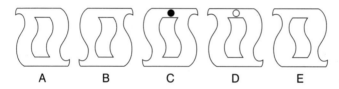

A   B   C   D   E

37. expert is to maven as novice is to: votary, sibling, tyro, boffin, scholar

38. What is the longest word that can be produced from the following 10 letters?

MUERVHANYL

39. What number should replace the question mark?

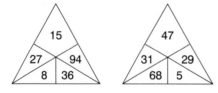

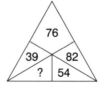

40.

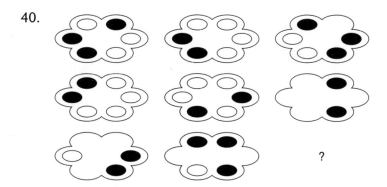

?

Which figure should replace the question mark?

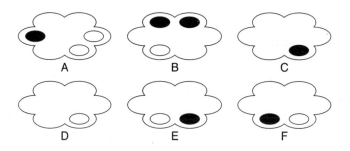

A   B   C

D   E   F

Questions

1.

Which is the missing section?

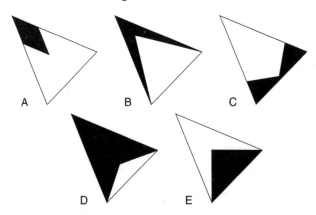

2. Add one letter, not necessarily the same letter, to the beginning, middle or end of each of these words to form two other words that are similar in meaning.

tip   aunt

3. What letter comes next?

   A   D   H   K   O   ?

4. What numbers should replace the question marks?

   5   3   8   1   2   5
   7   2   2   4   9   3
   2   5   6   5   ?   ?

5.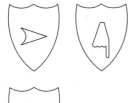

   Which is the missing shield?

   A   B   C   D   E

6. CUBED RESULT is an anagram of which two words that are opposite in meaning?

7. surmise is to conjecture as axiom is to: custom, idea, concept, caprice, premise

8. What number should replace the question mark?

   18   6   15   9
   13   11   7   17
    5   19   ?   3
   16   8   14   10

9.

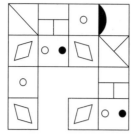

Which is the missing segment?

 A   B   C

 D   E   F

10. Which is the odd one out?

lampoon, pillory, spoof, burlesque, skit

11. Which two rhyming words mean the same as
    DELIGHTFUL OFFERING?

12. What number should replace the question mark?

3925 : 277

4697 : 2416

6257 : ?

13.

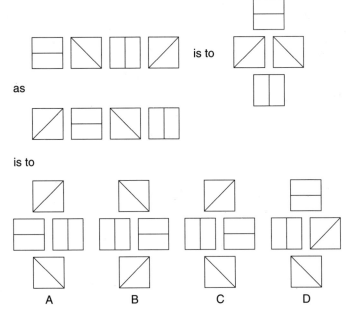

is to

as

is to

A	B	C	D

14. Which of the following is not an anagram of a musical term?

no baiter   rent coco   revue rot   rod arch   shop yard

15. Insert the missing number in each grid.

3	9	6	7
4	9		6
3	4	8	8
2	7	4	9

7	9	3	4
9	8	5	2
6	9	7	6
5	4	9	

16.

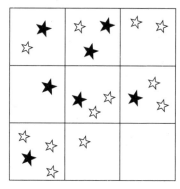

Which is the missing square?

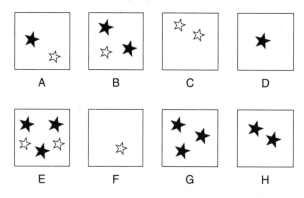

17. NICE OLD NOUN is an anagram of which familiar phrase (two, five, four letters).

Clue: the height of bliss?

18. Kate has a quarter as many again as Peter and Peter has a third as many again as Jill. Altogether they have 120. How many has each?

19. Change one letter only in each word to produce a familiar phrase.

so dive I dot O bid came

20.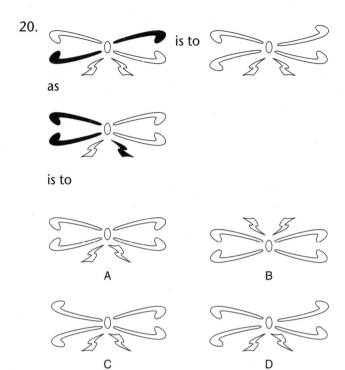

21. What number should replace the question mark?

1		1			2	3	2
	4			2			3
2		2			2		2
	4			2			3
	3	5	3			4	3
	3		3		3	?	
1			2		3		2
		1				2	

22.

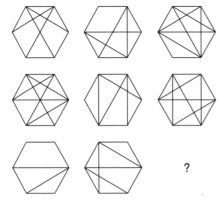

Which hexagon should replace the question mark?

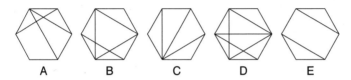

A   B   C   D   E

23. Restore the vowels to the row of letters below to spell out four words that are similar in meaning. All consonants are in the correct order.

D R C H R S H V N R T R V R

24. Insert the missing letters to spell out a familiar phrase reading clockwise. Only alternate letters are shown and you must find the starting point.

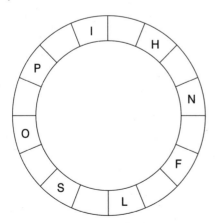

25.

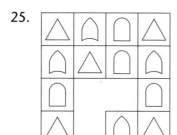

Which is the missing segment?

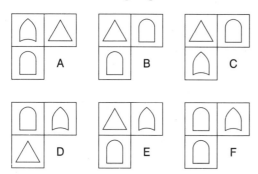

26. Find two words, one reading clockwise round one circle and the other anticlockwise round the other circle, which are antonyms. You must find the starting points and provide the missing letters.

27. Only one set of five letters below can be rearranged to spell out a five-letter English word. Find the word.

GOZAM   TROMC   PLACT   OECLR   MUYJP   TANRO   EFOLC

28. How many minutes is it before 12 noon if 90 minutes ago it was twice as many minutes past 8 am?

29.

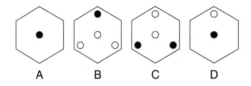

Which hexagon should replace the question mark?

A   B   C   D

30. Which is the odd one out?

   drapes, realtor, fanlight, diaper, tuxedo

31. A   B   C   D   E   F   G   H

   Which letter is two to the right of the letter immediately to the left of
   the letter three to the right of the letter immediately to the right of the
   letter A?

32. What numbers should replace the question marks?

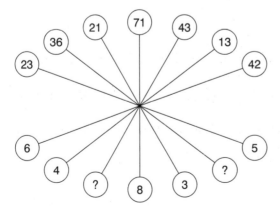

33.
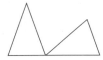

Which of the options below continues the above sequence?

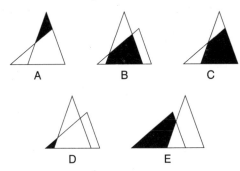

34. patella is to kneecap as sternum is to: collarbone, jawbone, thighbone, breastbone, shoulder-blade.

35. Start at one of the corner squares and spiral clockwise round the perimeter to spell out a nine-letter word, finishing at the centre. You must provide the missing letters.

N   I   N

E   *   S

*   L   U

36. If Tony's age + Cherie's age = 80 and Tony's age + Gordon's age = 98 and Cherie's age + Gordon's age = 94, how old are Tony, Cherie and Gordon?

37. Which is the odd one out?

38. Which of the following is not an anagram of an animal?

    one leapt   take choir   the plane   trap hen   leg laze

39. Out of 100 women surveyed leaving Harrods, 83 had a white bag, 77 had black shoes, 62 carried an umbrella and 95 wore a ring. What is the minimum number of women who must have had all four items?

40.

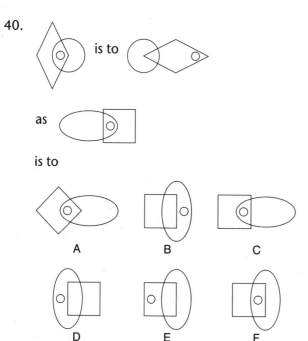

Questions

1. Which is the odd one out?

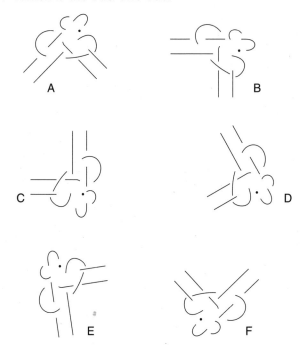

2. female is to nanny as male is to: Joey, Tommy, Harry, Billy, Larry

3. Change one letter only in each word to produce a familiar phrase.
   tin fog cat

4. What number should replace the question mark?

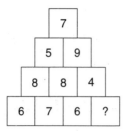

5.

What comes next?

A

B

C

D

E

6. Which is the odd one out?

   calypso, concerto, aria, shanty, madrigal

7. Insert a word in the brackets that has the same meanings as the definitions either side of the brackets.

   ascend (– – – – –) calibration

8. I picked a basket full of apples from my orchard. By the time I arrived home, I had given away 75 per cent to my son, 0.625 of the remainder to my son's neighbour and then eaten one of the remainder. I arrived home with just two apples. How many apples did I originally pick from my orchard?

9. How many lines appear below?

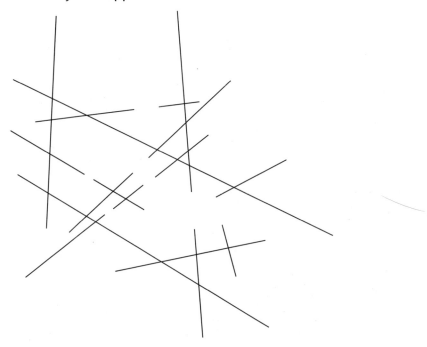

10. Which word in brackets is most opposite in meaning to the word in capitals?

    KNACK (necessity, surplus, ineptitude, facility, quell)

11. Solve the anagram in brackets (11 letters) to complete the quotation by Frank Crane.

    Your soul (ironic button) to the sum of things is yourself.

12. What number should replace the question mark?

4	2	3	2	5	4
6	7	5	1	7	3
5	1	3	?	6	5

13. Which is the odd one out?

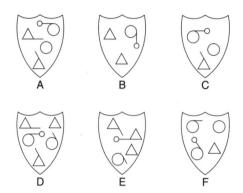

14. Fit the four-letter words into the crossword.

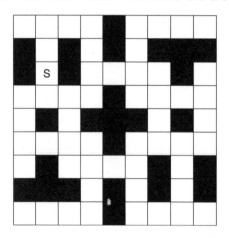

ATOM NOSY COOL LAMP YAWN MAIN SHIP EAST KING VETO PEAK
UNIT DARK ZEST ZEAL UNDO STAG TAKE TAME SUCH

15. Which four numbers should complete the grid?

2	4	8	3	9	2	4
9	8	3	9	2	4	8
3	4			9	8	3
8	2			2	3	9
4	9	3	8	4	9	2
2	9	3	8	4	2	4
3	8	4	2	9	3	8

16.

Which is the missing segment?

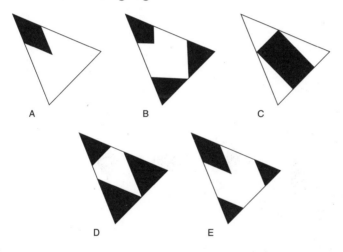

A   B   C

D   E

17. Place a word in the bracket that creates another word or phrase when tacked onto the end of the first word, and creates another word or phrase when placed in front of the second word.

stone (– – – –) feet

18. What numbers should go on the bottom line?

3   6   9   15
8   2   10   12
11   8   19   27
19   10   29   39
?   ?   ?   ?

19. Which two words are closest in meaning?

    coquetry, flippancy, apathy, adaptability, levity, celerity

20.

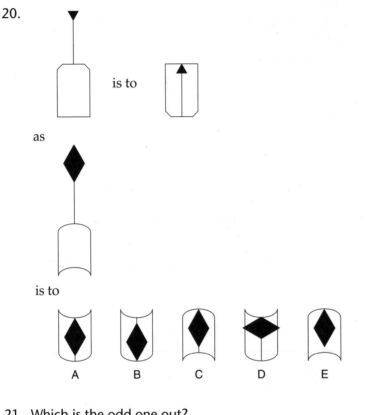

21. Which is the odd one out?

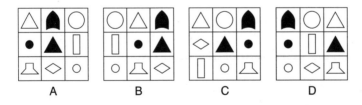

22. Change one letter only in each word to produce a familiar phrase.

    may do fan

23. exigent is to exacting as convoluted is to: esoteric, onerous, elusive, strenuous, intricate

24. What weighs most: something that weighs 60 kg plus one-sixth of its own weight, or something that weighs 46 kg plus one-third of its own weight?

25.

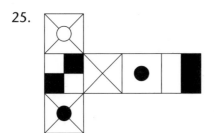

When the above is folded to form a cube, just one of the following can be produced. Which one?

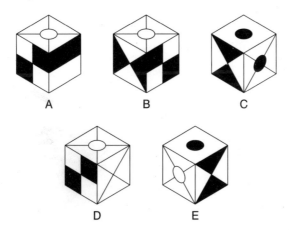

A   B   C

D   E

26. Which is the odd one out?

optimize, retrograde, ameliorate, regenerate, enhance

27. What number continues the sequence?

25, 50, 27, 46, 31, 38, 39, ?

28. Insert a word in the brackets that means the same as the definitions either side of the brackets.

protracted (– – – –) desire

29.

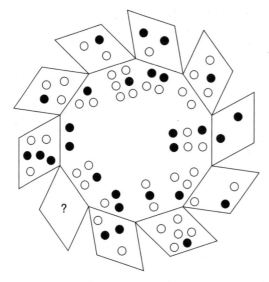

What should replace the question mark?

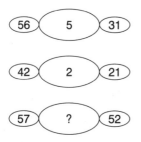

A	B	C	D	E

30. What number should replace the question mark?

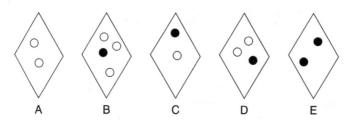

31. What is the longest English word that can be produced from the following 10 letters?

NURDESBOTA

32. Which word in brackets is closest in meaning to the word in capitals?

RAMIFICATION (uproar, regulation, collision, consequence, stronghold)

33. Which is the odd one out?

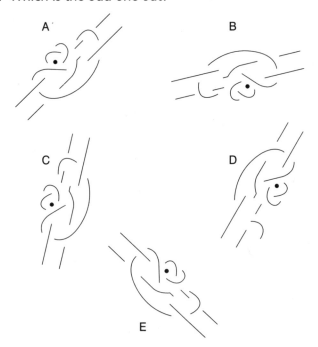

34. What number should replace the question mark?

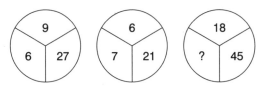

35. Place a word in the bracket that creates another word or phrase when tacked onto the end of the first word, and creates another word or phrase when placed in front of the second word.

march (– – – –) master

36.

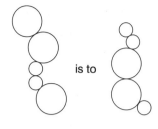

is to

as

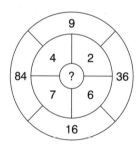

is to

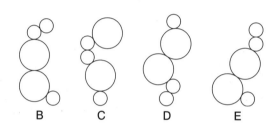

A   B   C   D   E

37. What number should replace the question mark?

```
           9
      4  |  2
  84 ----?---- 36
      7  |  6
          16
```

38. UNMARKED SEATS is an anagram of which familiar phrase (four, two, seven letters)?

Clue: sharp

39. Which two of these words are most opposite in meaning?

quaint, allegorical, excellent, factual, bellicose, overt

40. Which is the odd one out?

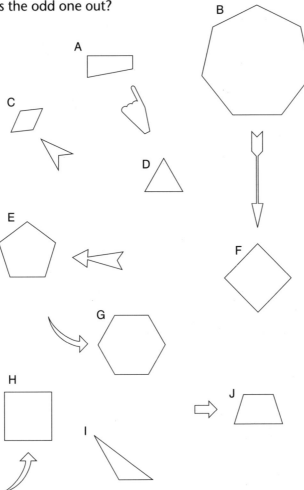

1. Which word in brackets is closest in meaning to the word in capitals?
   IRREFUTABLE (lost, sure, wise, secure, optimal)

2.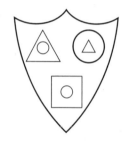

   Which shield below is most like the shield above?

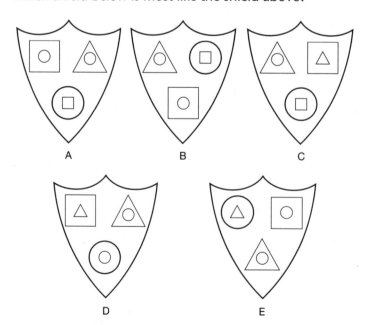

3. Insert three body parts (each three letters long) into the gaps to complete the words below:

   W _ _ _ Y
   E _ _ _ Y
   T _ _ _ E

4. What number should replace the question mark?

7	5	6	6
5	4	3	4
2	9	4	?

5. Which is the odd one out?

   transcend, cascade, plummet, subside, prolapse

6.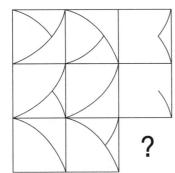

   Which square should replace the question mark?

   A   B   C   D   E

7. Only one of the following groups of five letters can be arranged to form an English five-letter word. Can you find the word?

   MURDC
   BEWAP
   UNREL
   YIGEN
   THABL

8. Insert a word in the brackets that means the same as the definitions outside the brackets.

   lightly-built (   ) give offence to

9. A train travelling at a speed of 90 mph enters a tunnel 3.5 miles long. The length of the train is 0.25 miles. How long does it take for all of the train to pass through the tunnel, from the moment the front enters to the moment the rear emerges?

10. auri- is to gold as argent- is to:
    brass, steel, emerald, silver, aluminium

11.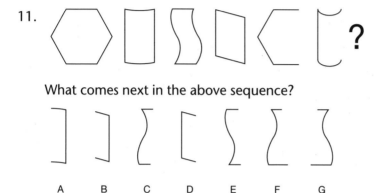

    What comes next in the above sequence?

    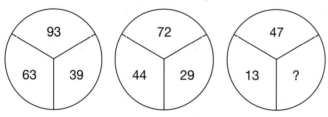

    A   B   C   D   E   F   G

12. What number should replace the question mark?

    93   63   39   72   44   29   47   13   ?

13. Which phrase in brackets is opposite to the phrase in capitals?

    AS A RULE (out of turn, hardly ever, out of date, rough-and-ready, now and again)

14. What number should replace the question mark?

2	7

9	3	7

| | 6 | 6 |

| | | 5 |

9	4

6	2	?

| | 7 | 2 |

| | | 3 |

15. In the sequence below, which letter is two to the right of the letter immediately to the left of the letter three to the right of the letter two to the left of the letter D?

    A B C D E F G H

16. Which is the odd one out?

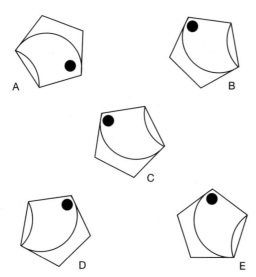

17. What letter should replace the question mark?

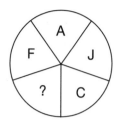

18. What phrase is suggested by the arrangement of letters below?

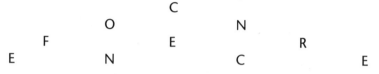

19. Which word when inserted in the brackets will complete the first word and start the second?

IMP (_ _ _) EAR

20. Harbour is to shelter as nurture is to:

shield, rear, secure, pamper, immunize

21. What is the meaning of fastigate?
    a. doubled
    b. slippery
    c. closed
    d. like a pyramid
    e. 5-barred gate

22. Place two three-letter bits together to make a six-letter word.

ING ETS LOW LIN DAF SWA MER NER ROB ODI

Clue: bird.

23. All of the vowels are missing from this trite saying, 'Hood's Warning'. Can you replace them?

BSRTH   BRNSN   GGDBF   RPTTN   GTHMT   HNGR

24. What four-letter word is missing in this list?

palm
mast
tory

_ _ _ _

ante
earn
nose

25. Which number should replace the question mark?

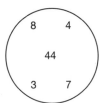 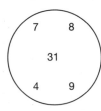 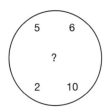

26. See if you can rearrange these words to make a trite saying.

LIBRARY	A	LIKE	BY
TO	READ	A	COLLECT
WOMAN	HE	TIME	CAN
IS	THE	TOO	A
MAN	A	BOOK	OLD

27.

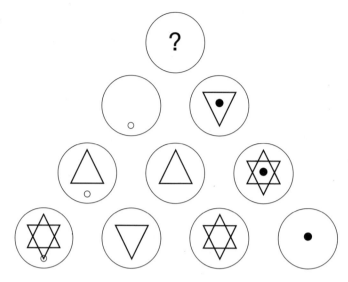

Which circle should replace the question mark?

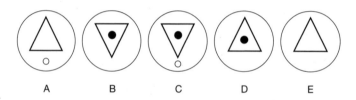

A   B   C   D   E

28. Identify a number in the grid that meets the two following simple rules:

   a. It is not in any line across that contains a square.

   b. It is not in any line down that contains a prime number.

23	36	8	48
7	6	13	16
15	21	3	5
18	25	4	12

29. Fill in the blanks to find a word.

30. What have all of these words in common?

pond
toga
seal
find
joan
spin

31. Place two four-letter bits together to make an eight-letter word.

PEDI BURT GIGA FRAI ETIK NTIC PHON LING CUBB LICY

32. What number should replace the question mark?

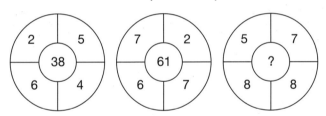

33. Fill in the letters to spell out two fish of six letters.

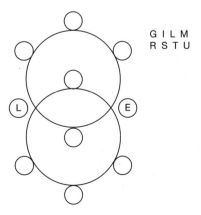

G I L M
R S T U

34.

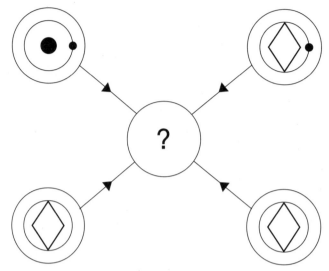

Each line and symbol that appears in the four outer circles, above, is transferred to the centre circle according to these rules. If a line or symbol occurs in the outer circles:

once: it is transferred
twice: it is possibly transferred
3 times: it is transferred
4 times: it is not transferred

Which of the circles A, B, C, D or E, shown below, should appear at the centre of the diagram, above?

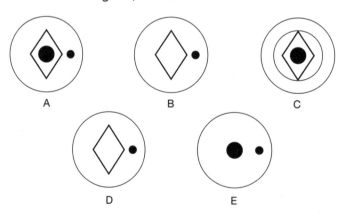

35.

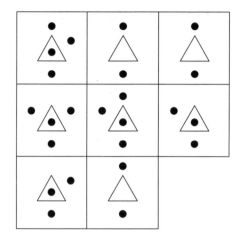

Which is the missing square?

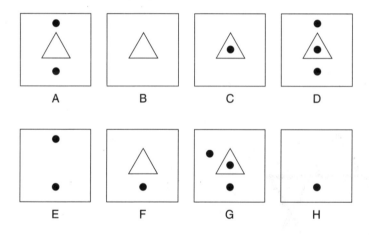

A   B   C   D

E   F   G   H

36. Replace the vowels to form a word:

CRPC

37. What is an orris?

a. pepper
b. horse
c. flower
d. architrave

38. Insert a word in the brackets that means the same as the words outside the brackets.

GEM (_ _ _ _ _) DUNG BEETLE

39. Which one of B will not fit into A to make six-letter words?

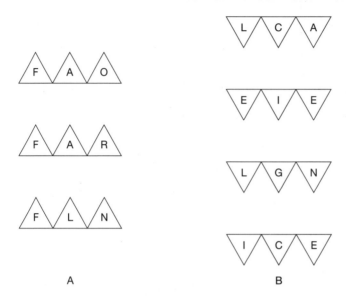

40. Find a boxing term made up of six letters outside the star and six letters inside the star.

1. How many minutes is it before 12 noon if 15 minutes ago it was four times as many minutes past 9 am?

2. If meat in a river (3 in 6) is T(ham)es, find a word meaning contented in a country (4 in 10).

3. Which two words are most alike in meaning?
   boycott, litigate, proscribe, sanction, postulate, intend

4.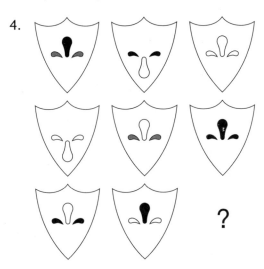

Which shield should replace the question mark?

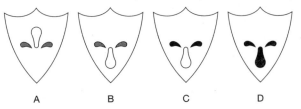

A   B   C   D

5. 'How many steps to the top of the Eiffel Tower?' asked the tourist. '896 steps plus half the number of steps,' replied the gendarme. How many steps are there to the top of the Eiffel Tower?

6. Complete the three words so that the last two letters of the first word are the first two letters of the second word, the last two letters of the second word are the first two letters of the third word, and the last two letters of the third word are the first two letters of the first word, thus completing the circle:

   _ _ M P _ _
   _ _ M I _ _
   _ _ G A _ _

7. Which two words that sound alike but are spelt differently mean pure/hunted?

8.

   is to: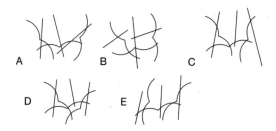

   as:

   is to:

9. Which is the odd one out?

   artful, astute, shifty, devious, guileful

10. Insert the letters of the phrase: RAVISH TAIL once each only into the blanks to complete two words which mean the same as the words above them:

   wait   pertinent
   _E_ _T_ _E   _E_ _T_ _E

11. Which two letters should replace the question mark?

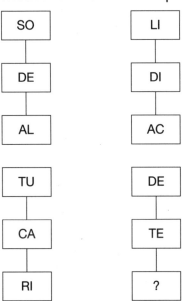

12. What number should replace the question mark?

   72   (68)   41
   28   (98)   16
   34   (??)   56

13. Martinmas is to November as Candlemas is to:

   January, February, March, October, December

14. A well-known phrase has been divided into groups of three letters that have then been placed in the wrong order. Find the phrase.

   EST HON OBI LTW ONE RDS WIT KIL

15. Find one word in List B that should be placed with the words in List A to replace the question mark.

List A	List B
tape	chip
wood	bell
wine	card
deer	bottle
flag	note
?	

16.

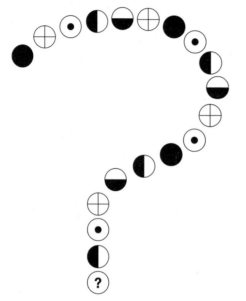

Which circle below should replace the circle with the question mark?

A   B   C   D   E

17. Which two words are the odd ones out?

end	use	domains	precast
rub	can	sadness	met
ace	suburbs	panache	ice
presume	special	attempt	aim

18. What number should replace the question mark?

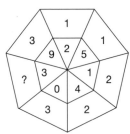

19. Which word in brackets is opposite to the word in capitals?

    MOTLEY (sensible, uniform, smooth, sweet, saturnine)

20. Which is the odd one out?

21. What is a lateen?

    a. a musical instrument
    b. a bishop's hat
    c. a sail
    d. a bird

22.

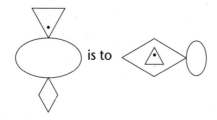 is to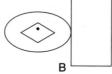

as

is to

A

B

C   D   E

23.

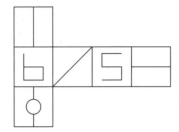

When the above is folded to form a cube, which is the only one of the following that *cannot* be produced?

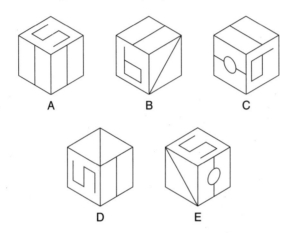

A   B   C

D   E

24. Find the missing letters to make a word.

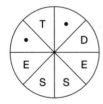

25. Fill in the letters to make two dogs of six letters each.

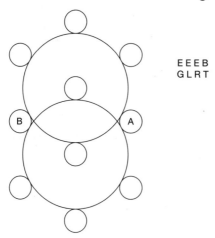

E E E B
G L R T

26. What number should replace the question mark?

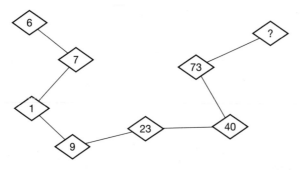

27.

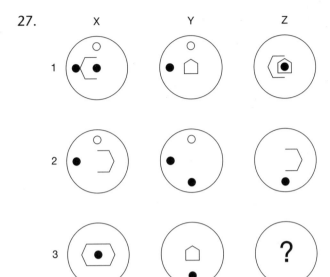

Which letter should replace the question mark to a definite rule?

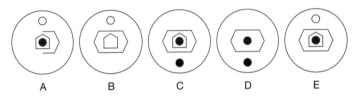

28. Which of the following is always associated with entrecote?

    a. eels
    b. cream
    c. rice
    d. steak

29. All the vowels have been removed from this trite saying, 'Sukhomlinov's Law'.

    THMST BRLLN TLYDR SSDRM YWLLS LLYLS

30. What do all of these words have in common?

    calmness
    undefended
    firstly
    sighing
    disturb

31. What five-letter word can be placed in front of each of these words to make new words?

_ _ _ _ _ BIRD
_ _ _ _ _ CLUB
_ _ _ _ _ FALL
_ _ _ _ _ JAR
_ _ _ _ _ SCHOOL

32. What number should replace the question mark?

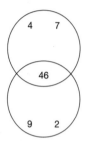 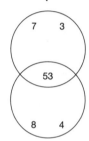 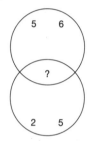

33. Find the 10-letter word by moving from circle to circle; each circle must only be used once.

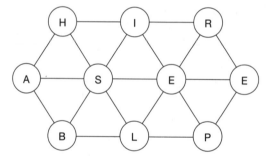

34.

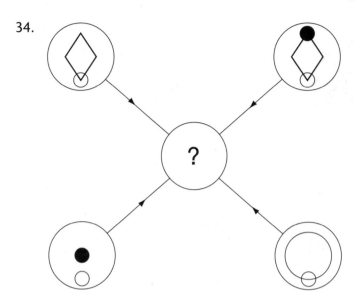

Each line and symbol that appears in the four outer circles, above, is transferred to the centre circle according to these rules. If a line or symbol occurs in the outer circles:

once: it is transferred
twice: it is possibly transferred
3 times: it is transferred
4 times: it is not transferred

Which of the circles A, B, C, D or E, shown below, should appear at the centre of the diagram, above?

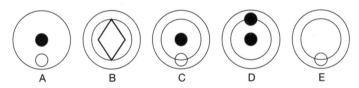

35.

Which is the missing segment?

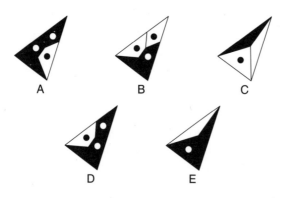

36. Find a one-word anagram for PETES LAD.

37. Place two three-letter bits together to make a six-letter word.
ICE MER RIN SAR SAL WHA PLA DIN LER MAN
Clue: fish

38. Which of the following is not a boat?
    a. brougham
    b. frigate
    c. barque
    d. cutter
    e. dromond

39. What familiar phrase is represented below?

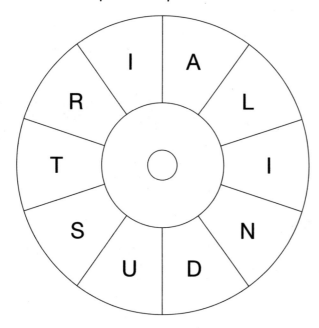

40. Fill in the blanks to find an eight-letter word.

_A_R_D_N

Questions

1.

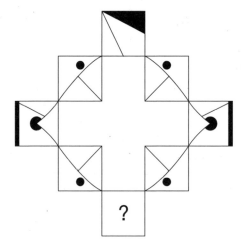

Which square below should replace the question mark?

A   B   C   D   E

2. What number should replace the question mark?

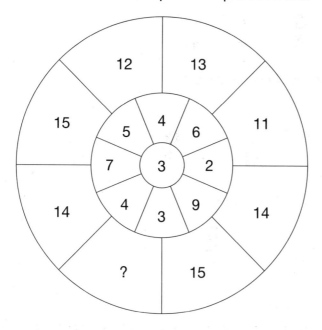

3. Which of the following is not an anagram of a type of dog?
    LOOPED
    NO SLAM
    BAG EEL
    SAIL UK
    BASTES

4. Consider the following list of words:

    mountain, wine, spoon, tennis

    Now choose just one of the following words which has something specific in common with them:

    Saturday, friendship, manners, hope, chant

5.

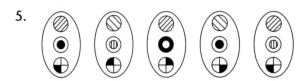

What comes next in the above sequence?

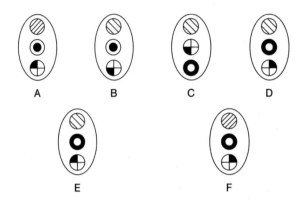

6. Find the starting point and track along the connecting lines from letter to letter to spell out a well-known phrase (3, 2, 4, 5).

   Note: when travelling from letter to letter along a side of a triangle, lines may have to pass through letters that are not part of the solution.

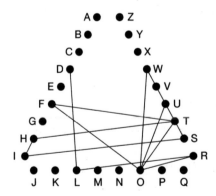

7. Which word, when inserted in the brackets, will complete the first word and start the second?

   High (   ) beat

8. Change one letter only from each word to form a well-known phrase.

   ail sands of neck

9. Which is the odd number out in each square?

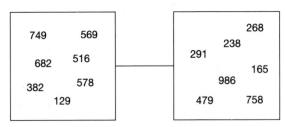

10. What three-letter word can be placed after each of the following to form five English words?

F _ _ _
H _ _ _
P _ _ _
CH _ _ _
FL _ _ _

11.   is to:

as

is to:

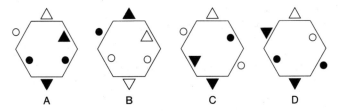

   A   B   C   D

12. What is *meerschaum*?

   a. hard white mineral
   b. a prayer said at dawn
   c. a nerve-racking experience
   d. way of living
   e. a carved figure

13. What number should replace the question mark?

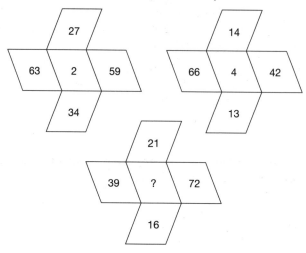

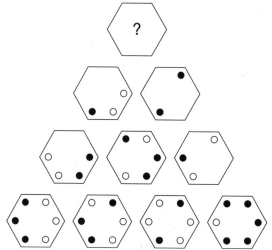

14.

Which hexagon should replace the question mark?

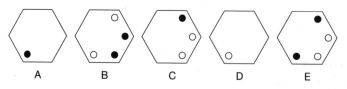

A   B   C   D   E

15. Insert the missing letters to find two words that form a phrase:

    T O D C O D R C N T E

       –

       –

    _ _ _ _ U _ _ _ _

       –

    Clue: harmonic excursion

16. Which two words are most alike in meaning?

    discipline, schism, blister, snatch, rift, signal

17. Which two words are most opposite in meaning?

    edacious, reserved, clean, rough, generous, anomalous

18. Which number should replace the question mark?

```
              1
        2           2
    2       1           5
3       1       2           9
    2       3       3
        2       3
            ?
```

19. Mule is to slipper as sabot is to:

    shoe, boot, moccasin, sandal, clog

20. Which is the odd one out?

    quick, curt, rapid, swift, fleet

21. What is the meaning of mantua?
    a. hat
    b. animal
    c. gown
    d. insect

22. What is the next number in this series?

    $\frac{1}{2}$, $\frac{2}{3}$, $\frac{8}{9}$, $1\frac{5}{27}$, ?

23. hedonism is to pleasure as aestheticism is to:

    morality, beauty, ideas, perception, reality

24. Place two four-letter bits together to equal an eight-letter word.

    CONT PINE LLON BANT INUI EFFI CALA DINE TERA PAPI

25. What number should replace the question mark?

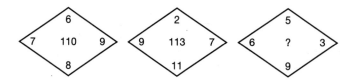

26. Fill in the letters to make two animals of six letters.

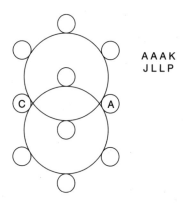

AAAK
JLLP

27.

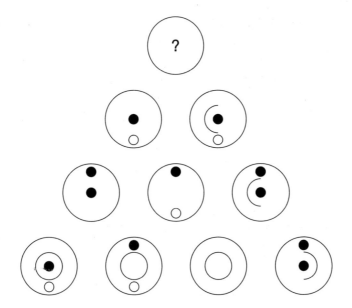

Which circle should replace the question mark?

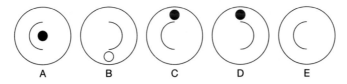

A   B   C   D   E

28. What is a hacienda?

   a. a plant
   b. a village
   c. a range of mountains
   d. a ranch
   e. a dance

29. All of the vowels have been removed from this trite saying by Judith Cohen. See if you can replace them.

   WLLMT LLJRH DHDCH S

30. What does nescient mean?

   a. agreeable
   b. hard of hearing
   c. ignorant
   d. hesitant

31. What is the next number in this series?

$1/4$, $3/8$, $9/16$, $27/32$, $1^{17}/64$, ?

32. Which circle cannot be made into a word?

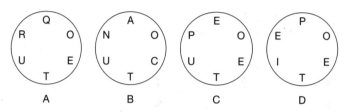

A   B   C   D

33. Fill in the blanks and find two words that are synonyms.

34.

Each line and symbol that appears in the four outer circles, above, is transferred to the centre circle according to these rules. If a line or symbol occurs in the outer circles:

once: it is transferred
twice: it is possibly transferred
3 times: it is transferred
4 times: it is not transferred

Which of the circles A, B, C, D or E, shown below, should appear at the centre of the diagram, above?

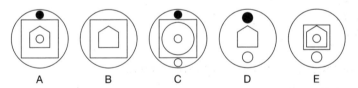

| A | B | C | D | E |

35.

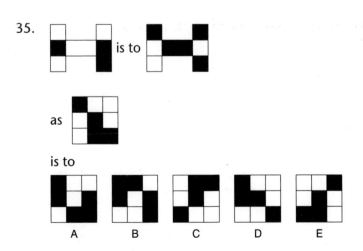

is to

as

is to

| A | B | C | D | E |

36.

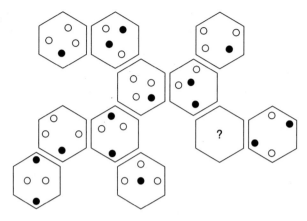

Which hexagon should replace the question mark?

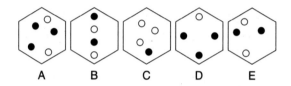

A   B   C   D   E

37. Which of the following is not a nautical term?

   a. RANIME
   b. CRANOH
   c. EBONAC
   d. YEHCOK
   e. YAPIRC

38. Find the number to replace the question mark.

   8, 10, 9¾, 8¼, 11½, 6½, ?

39. Find a 10-letter word by travelling from circle to circle.

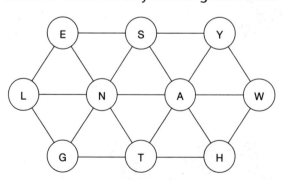

40. Find the longest word in the square by moving from letter to letter in any direction, but each letter must be used only once.

B	X	W	O	S
I	Q	U	R	K
C	T	E	J	L
P	V	H	M	Y
F	A	G	D	N

Questions

1. How many circles contain a black dot?

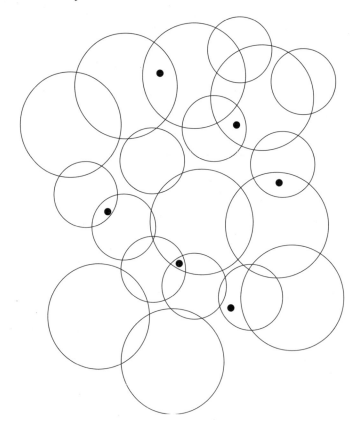

2. Which is the odd one out?

   anther, flower, stigma, petal, nectar

3. Complete the bottom line of numbers.

7	4	9	2
11	16	9	13
22	20	24	25
?	?	?	?

4. Insert the word in brackets that means the same as the definitions outside the brackets.

    game bird (   ) cower

5. Which two rhyming words mean: fresh hint?

6.

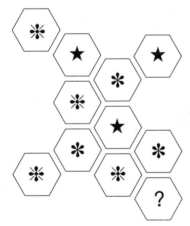

    Which symbol should replace the question mark?

    A   B   C

7. Which of the following is not an anagram of the word:
   ANAGRAMMATICALLY?

   MANIACALLY TAG ARM
   ILL MAY MAGNA CARTA
   CLARITY AN AMALGAM
   TINY MAGICAL ALARM
   A MAGICAL MANLY ART
   ARM MANLY GALACTICA
   MY A CARNAL MAIL TAG
   ARMY GALA CLAIMANT
   ALARMING MALAY CAT

8. What number continues the following sequence?

   759, 675, 335, 165, ?

9. Find the starting point and read clockwise to find a familiar phrase
   (5 2 3 6). Only alternate letters are shown.

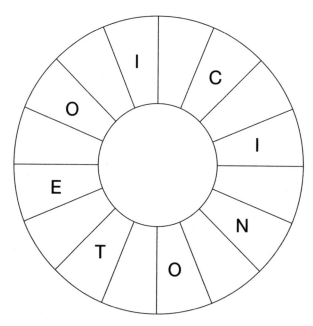

10. Which two words are most opposite in meaning?

   politician, principal, miscreant, subsidiary, practice, prosecutor

11.

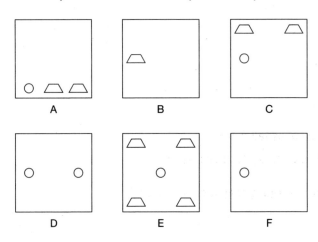

Which square below should replace the question mark?

A

B

C

D

E

F

12. Complete the numbers in the final column.

15	20	19	20
14	23	9	?
5	15	24	?

13. Which word is the odd one out?

auctioneers, executioner, postponed, erroneously, weaponless

14. What numbers should replace the question marks?

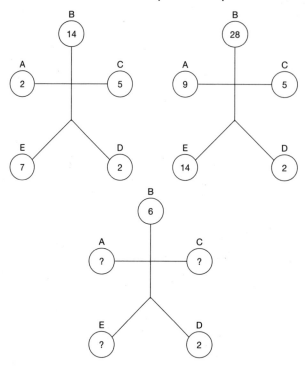

15. succeed is to prevail as fail is to:

contrive, agonize, destroy, founder, grovel

16. What letter should replace the question mark?

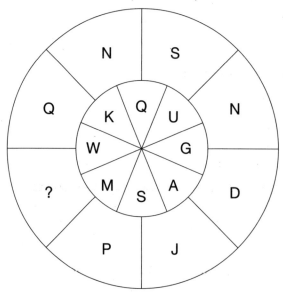

17. Solve the clues to find four six-letter words. The same three letters appear in each word, which are represented by XYZ below. XYZ is a familiar three-letter word.

XYZ _ _ _   most venerable
_ XYZ _ _   turned over
_ _ XYZ _   castigates
_ _ _ XYZ   defend

18.

What comes next in the above sequence?

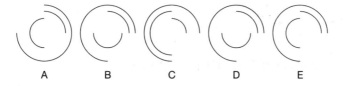

A   B   C   D   E

19. Which two words are most alike in meaning?

waspish, jovial, peppery, prudent, perilous, lewd

20. A car travels the first half of a motorway journey at an average speed of 40 mph, and the second half of the journey at an average speed of 60 mph. What is the average speed for the entire journey?

21. Letters are traced across the circle by chords. If the next letter is four letters or less away it will be found by tracing around the circumference.

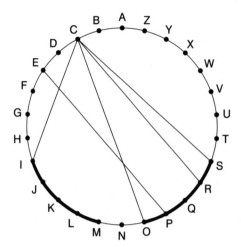

Clue: MAKES THINGS LARGER BUT IT IS SMALL
(10 letters)

22. Place two three-letter bits together to make a six-letter word.

GER BOL EPR GER TLY BAL SHE BAD CAT TIG

Clue: animal

23. What is the meaning of kibble?
    a. iron bucket
    b. card game
    c. a quarrel
    d. fruit

24. Which is the odd one out?

midge
bassoon
solemn
dabbled
brilliant
coding
carpet

25. Fill in the letters to make two birds of six letters.

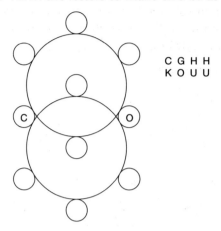

C G H H
K O U U

26. What familiar phrase is suggested below?

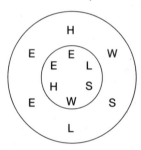

27. Each of the nine squares in the grid marked 1A to 3C should incorporate all the lines and symbols that are shown in the squares of the same letter and number immediately above and to the left. For example, 2B should incorporate all the lines and symbols that are in 2 and B.

One of the squares is incorrect? Which one is it?

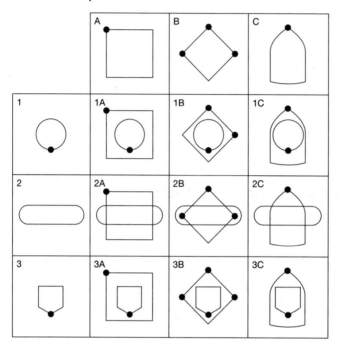

28. Which four-letter word can be placed in front of all of these words to make new words?

_ _ _ _ BAKED
_ _ _ _ BOILED
_ _ _ _ BOARD
_ _ _ _ BACK
_ _ _ _ HEADED

29. Fill in the missing vowels to make a trite saying.

THDMM   RTHLG   HTTHG   RTRTH   SCNDL

30. What is a jacana?

    a. bird
    b. fish
    c. insect
    d. animal

31. Which of the following is not a bird?

    a. TCTALE
    b. RYCANA
    c. NIRMEL
    d. FIFPUN
    e. ETIPEW

32. What number should replace the question mark?

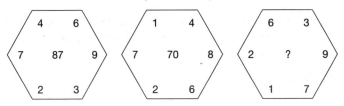

33. Find the missing letters to make a word.

34.

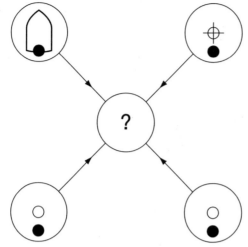

Each line and symbol that appears in the four outer circles, above, is transferred to the centre circle according to these rules. If a line or symbol occurs in the outer circles:

once: it is transferred
twice: it is possibly transferred
3 times: it is transferred
4 times: it is not transferred

Which of the circles A, B, C, D or E shown below should appear at the centre of the diagram, above?

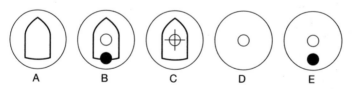

35. What do these words have in common?

  a. alone
  b. hold
  c. anger
  d. mask
  e. force

36. Find a one-word anagram for PAUL RICE.

37. Place two four-letter bits together to equal an eight-letter word.

    COCH, MAND, GERM, TONS, HLEA, LOCY, FRAC,
    TROC, ITES, IDIO

38. What have these words in common?

    cashed
    helmet
    soaking
    sublime
    plummet

39. Fill in the blanks to find two words that are antonyms.

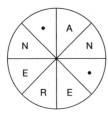 

40. Since my birth I have had a birthday cake with candles, one for each year of my birthday, each year.

    To date, I have had 325 candles. How old am I?

Questions

1. A statue is being carved by a sculptor. The original piece of marble weighed 250 kg. In the first week 30 per cent is cut away. In the second week 20 per cent of the remainder is cut away. In the thirdweek the statue is completed when 25 per cent of the remainder is cut away. What is the weight of the final statue?

2. Which word in brackets is closest in meaning to the word in capitals?

   ESPOUSAL (advocacy, suspicion, agreement, bias, honesty)

3. Which is the odd one out?

   relating
   triangle
   rambling
   integral
   altering

4. Which is the odd one out?

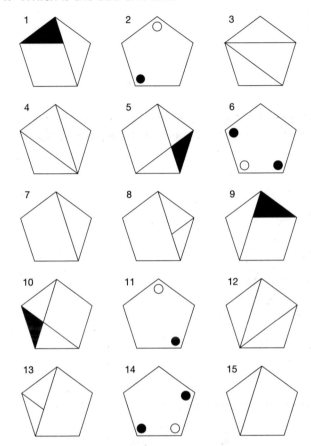

5. Which number is the odd one out?

159
248
963
357
951
852

6. Sunday
   Monday
   Tuesday
   Wednesday
   Thursday
   Friday
   Saturday

   What day is two days before the day immediately following the day three days before the day two days after the day immediately before Friday?

7.

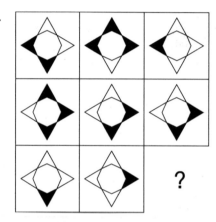

Which square should replace the question mark?

A

B

C   D

E   F

8. What is the longest English word that can be created from this set of letters, using each letter once only?

   NUHRIAKMTE

9. Apart from each having five letters, what do these words have in common?

   groom, spank, plaid, breve

10. Which is the odd one out?

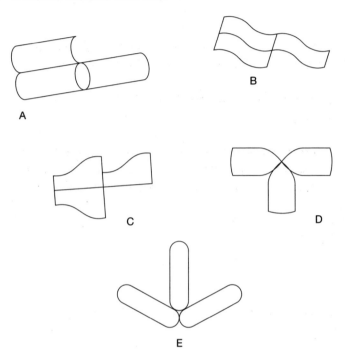

11. What four-digit number should replace the question mark?

   4342 (3176) 1726
   7995 (7516) 2162
   8418 (????) 1725

12. hypotenuse is to triangle as chord is to:

   polygon, cone, rhomboid, circle, heptagon

13. Insert the name of a type of fruit into the bottom line to complete nine three-letter words reading downwards.

A	S	P	C	R	O	F	M	C
R	I	E	A	U	D	O	A	O
_	_	_	_	_	_	_	_	_

14. Start at a corner letter and spiral clockwise round the perimeter, finish-ing at the centre letter, to spell out a nine-letter word. You have to provide the missing letters.

S   –   E
E   –   R
D   D   A

15. If meat in a river (3 in 6) is T(ham)es, can you find a word meaning *reconstitute* in the title of a Shakespeare play (6 in 7, 3, 7)?

16. Change one letter only from each word to form a well-known phrase.
    WE AIL ANY AND ILL

17. Find two eight-letter words, one reading clockwise round the inner circle, and the other reading anticlockwise round the outer circle, that are opposite in meaning. You have to provide the missing letters.

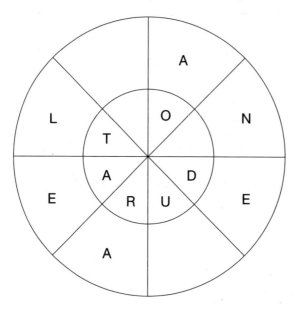

18.

What continues the above sequence?

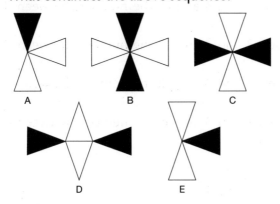

19. Use every letter of the newspaper headline below, once each only, to spell out three kinds of fish.

Nomad Robs Camel

20. What numbers should replace the question marks?

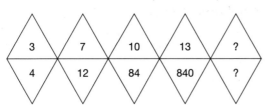

21.

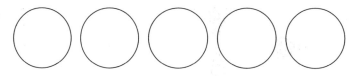

Place the numbers 1–5 in the circles so that:

the sum of the numbers 2 and 4 and all the numbers between them total 15;

the sum of the numbers 3 and 2 and all the numbers between them total 11;

the sum of the numbers 5 and 4 and all the numbers between them total 12;

the sum of the numbers 1 and 3 and all the numbers between them total 9.

22. Which is the odd one out in this list?

tackled
scarlet
grammar
godetia
stacking
starving

23. What is the next number in this sequence?

$7/8, -7/24, 7/72, -7/216$?

24. What is a pumpion?
a. drink
b. pumpkin
c. carriage
d. type of cheese

25. Find a 10-letter word moving from circle to circle. Each circle must only be used once.

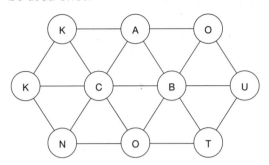

26.

EVERY	AND	IS	HILL
AGAINST	NO	WHICH	THE
WAY	ALWAYS	LUCK	TIME
YOU	BAD	JUST	RIDE
WIND	UP	MATTER	IT

Try to rearrange the above into a trite saying.

27.

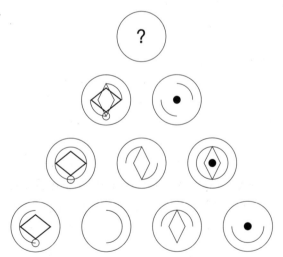

Which circle should replace the question mark?

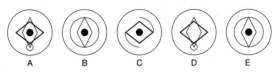

A   B   C   D   E

28. Which two words are opposite in meaning?

    severity, caution, incite, calm, impulse, wonder, stand, dismiss

29. Fill in the missing vowels to make a trite saying.

    FLSRS   HNWHR   FLSHV   BNBFR

30.

To which pentagon below can a dot be added so that it meets the same conditions as in the pentagon above?

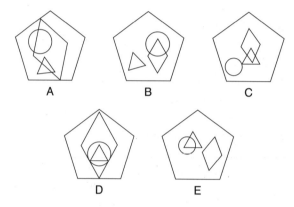

31. Which of the following is not a tree?

    LIOWWL
    CUPESR
    VATRAC
    CICAAA
    DODERA

32. Complete the words that are synonyms, clockwise or anticlockwise.

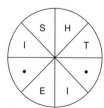 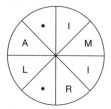

33. Place a word inside the brackets that means the same as the two words outside the brackets.

    SHEPHERD'S STAFF (_ _ _ _ _) ROGUE

34.
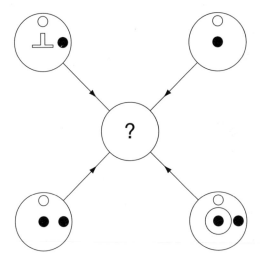

    Each line and symbol that appears in the four outer circles, above, is transferred to the centre circle according to these rules. If a line or symbol occurs in the outer circles:

    once: it is transferred
    twice: it is possibly transferred
    3 times: it is transferred
    4 times: it is not transferred

    Which of the circles, A, B, C, D or E shown below, should appear at the centre of the diagram, above?

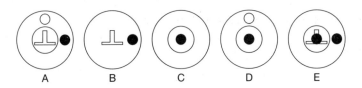

35. Which two words mean the same?

    bathos, spectacles, junta, carriage, archetype, cabal

36.

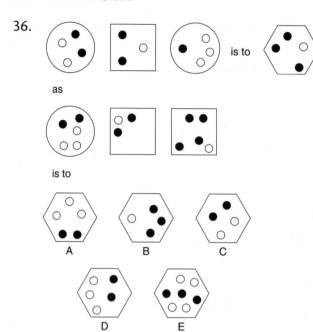

37. Which one of these was not a president of the United States?

RACRET
ROOVHE
PINCHAL
TAMRUN
SLIWNO

38. Which is the odd one out?

bazooka, shrapnel, claymore, harpoon, bonanza, arquebus

39. Fill in the blanks to find two words that are antonyms.

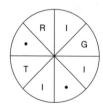

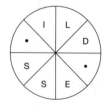

40. What number should replace the question mark?

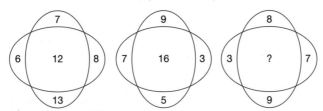

Questions

1. Which is the odd one out?

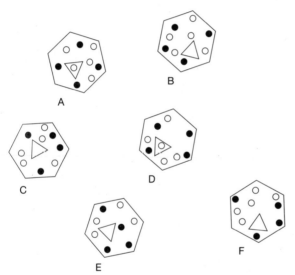

2. By starting at the Q in the centre and moving from letter to adjacent letter to an outside Z, how many different ways can the word QUIZ be spelt out?

```
            Z
        Z   I   Z
    Z   I   U   I   Z
Z   I   U   Q   U   I   Z
    Z   I   U   I   Z
        Z   I   Z
            Z
```

3. pediform is to foot as reniform is to:

   heart, kidney, tooth, beak, fingers

4. Which is the odd one out?

   pentad, limerick, quatrain, quincunx, pentagon

5. MOOD SLEEP

   The above is an anagram of which two words that are similar in meaning?

   Clue: sit still.

6. What letter should replace the question mark?

7. How many lines appear below?

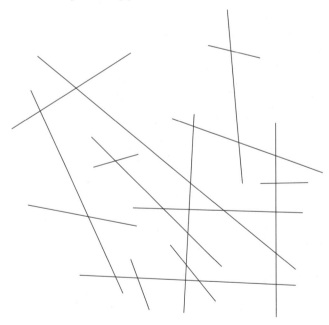

8. What is the length of line AB? (NB: Not to scale.)

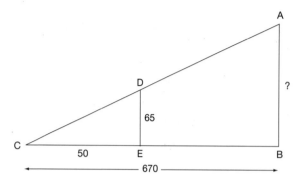

9. Complete the names of three animals by inserting the missing letters.

    _ A _ G _ R
    _ O _ K _ Y
    _ A _ B _ T

    Now rearrange the nine missing letters to find two words (6,3) in answer to the clue: *greased palms.*

10. Insert the following words into the grid below:

XENON	HOAX	PEA
ONION	HOLE	EWE
NINJA		DIG
NEWEL		SHY
LAUGH		DEW
SALON		OWE

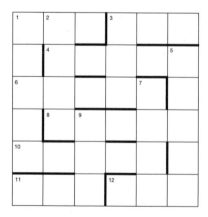

11.

?

What circle should replace the question mark?

A	B	C	D

12. What number should replace the question mark?

15	2	7	10
7	8	3	4
21	6	11	16
13	4	7	?

13. Which two rhyming words solve the following clue?

Sylvan flower seller

14. Which of the following is not an anagram of a type of ship?

ARK NET

LAY LEG

NUCHAL

BETASK

SPA MAN

15. Find the starting point and track along the connecting lines from letter to letter to spell out a well-known phrase (6, 2, 6).

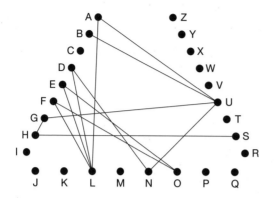

16.

is to

as

is to:

A   B   C

D   E

17. Which two words are most alike in meaning?
speech, hearsay, fury, boast, rumour, extract

18. Which is the odd number out?
9421, 7532, 9854, 8612, 6531, 8541

19. Find the starting point and fill in the blanks to find a familiar phrase (6, 6, 4) reading clockwise. Only alternate letters are shown.

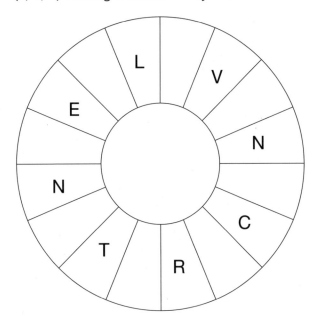

20. Change one letter only from each word to spell out a well-known phrase.

ACE FOUR ACE

21.

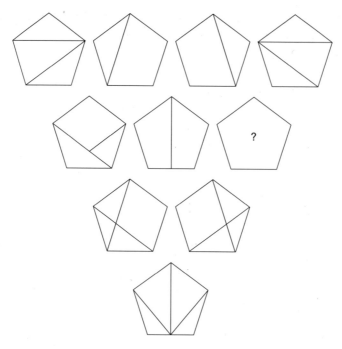

Which pentagon should replace the question mark?

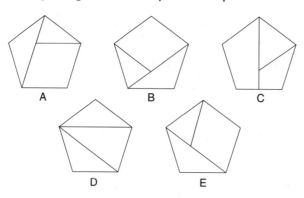

22. Which five-letter word can be placed in front of each of these words to make new words?

_ _ _ _ _ RUNNER
_ _ _ _ _ AGE
_ _ _ _ _ LINE
_ _ _ _ _ RANK
_ _ _ _ _ MAN

23.

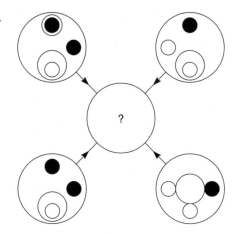

Each line and symbol that appears in the four outer circles above is transferred to the centre circle according to these rules: If a line or symbol occurs in the outer circles:

once:	it is transferred;
twice:	it is possibly transferred;
three times:	it is transferred;
four times:	it is not transferred.

Which of the circles A, B, C, D or E shown below should appear at the centre of the diagram above?

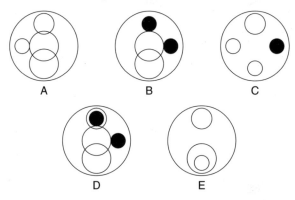

24. Place two three-letter bits together to equal an animal.

ONE, POL, VIC, ERA, BIS, UNA

25. Which circle cannot be made into a word?

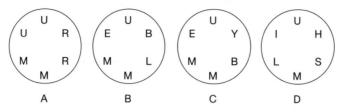

26. Fill in the blanks to find two words that are antonyms.

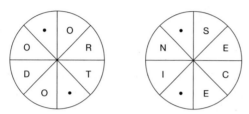

27.

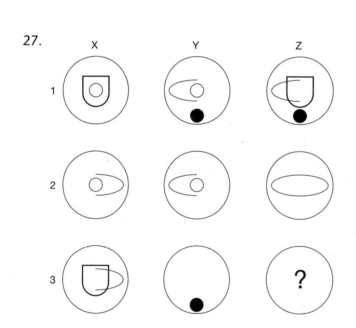

Which symbol should replace the question mark?

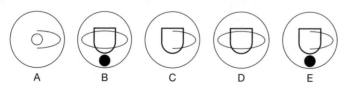

28. Which is the odd one out?

    timer
    loots
    repel
    times
    spots

29. Find a one-word anagram for SHOT PILL.

30. What is a plié?

    a. a climbing tool
    b. a ballet movement
    c. a pie
    d. a fencing stroke

31. What are the next two letters in this sequence?

    A, F, H, K, N, ?, ?

32. Fill in the blanks to find an eight-letter word.

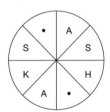

33. Fill in the blanks and find two words that are synonyms.

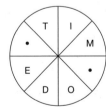 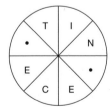

34.

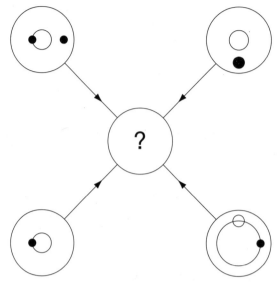

Each line and symbol that appears in the four outer circles, above, is transferred to the centre circle according to these rules. If a line or symbol occurs in the outer circles:

once: it is transferred
twice: it is possibly transferred
3 times: it is transferred
4 times: it is not transferred

Which of the circles A, B, C, D or E shown below should appear at the centre of the diagram, above?

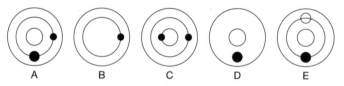

35. Find the missing vowels to make a trite saying.

WHNTH   BLLRN   GSTHR   HDBTT   RBSMS   PPR

36. Which of these is not an island?

LICSLY
NAGPEN
KENROY
DOLNON
YANMAC

37. Find a six-letter word using only these four letters: A, K, L, I.

38. Place two four-letter bits together to make an eight-letter word.
    RONI, DAMA, TION, RENI, POEN, PENT, AGOS, MACA, GADE, TICS

39. What number should replace the question mark?

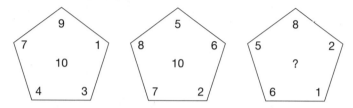

40. Find a 10-letter word by moving from circle to circle but you may only use each circle once.

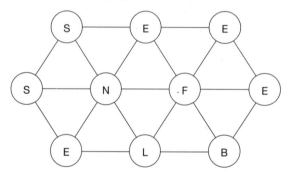

Questions

1. Which of the circles, A, B, C, D, E or F, should replace the question mark in the bottom large circle?

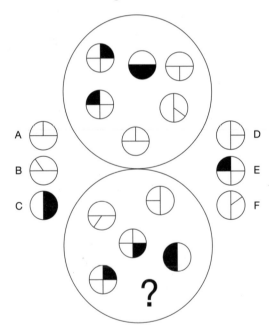

2. Change SEEK to FIND in three links by changing one letter at a time.

    SEEK

    _ _ _ _

    _ _ _ _

    _ _ _ _

    FIND

3. Six synonyms of the keyword SKILFUL are given. Take one letter in turn from each of these synonyms to spell out a further synonym of SKILFUL:

able, adept, dextrous, proficient, accomplished, competent

4. MUTINY (MILKY) MEEKLY

Using the same rules as above, what word is coded to go in the brackets below?

ALIGHT (_ _ _ _) BONNET

5. What number should replace the question mark?

```
                      7
               5            9
          8          8            4
       10         3          10        7
    1         ?          8         3          11
```

6. What letter should replace the question mark?

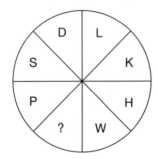

7.

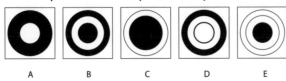

Which square should replace the question mark?

A   B   C   D   E

8. At a recent election, a total of 93,648 votes were cast for the four candidates, the winner exceeding his opponents by 25,627, 10,681 and 5,924 votes respectively. How many votes were cast for each candidate?

9. Which two letters come next in the following sequence?

A, D, I, P, Y, CF, DI, FD, ?

10. Insert the missing word:

DART   (STRANDED)   SEND
DINE   (DILIGENT)   ?

11. A B C D E F G H

What letter is two to the right of the letter immediately to the right of the letter two to the left of the letter three to the right of the letter immediately to the left of the letter E?

12.

13. Insert the word in brackets that means the same as the definitions outside the brackets.

    circuit (   ) splash

14. What number should replace the question mark?

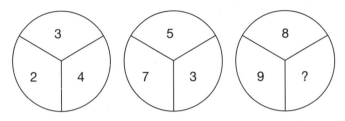

15. Find the starting point and track from letter to adjacent letter horizontally and vertically, but not diagonally, to spell out a 12-letter word. You have to provide the missing letters.

    ```
    _    E    E    _
    T    _    I    P
    A    L    R    E
    ```

16. What is the meaning of plenary?
    a. easy to bend
    b. overabundance
    c. able to absorb
    d. open to all
    e. acceptable

17. Change one letter only from each word to form a well-known phrase.

    TO LIVE NOT MAKES

18. Which two words are most alike in meaning?

    accommodate, bilk, score, chat, swindle, wind

19. What number should replace the question mark?
    ```
    4    7    3    8    9    2
    ?    9    0    2    5    1
    5    1    6    3    5    9
    ```

20.

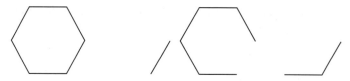

What comes next in the above sequence?

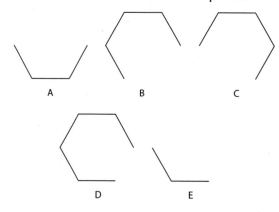

A   B   C

D   E

21. Which of the following is not clothing?
    a. togue
    b. hassock
    c. cassock
    d. chapeau

22. Fill in the missing vowels to find a trite saying.
    CLTTRD DSKMN FGNS

23. What is a picot?
    a. sword fish
    b. jewellery
    c. fabric
    d. loop of thread

24. Fill in the blanks to find two words that are synonyms (clockwise or anti-clockwise).

25. What familiar phrase is represented below?

PORTTAXUGAL

26. Find the missing letters to make a word.

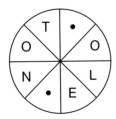

27. Each of the nine squares in the grid marked 1A to 3C should incorporate all the lines and symbols that are shown in the squares of the same
letter and number immediately above and to the left. For example, 2B
should incorporate all the lines and symbols that are in 2 and B.

One of the squares is incorrect. Which one is it?

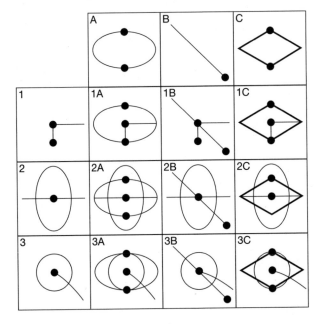

28. Solve the anagram to find a one-word answer.
    HEED LARKS.

29. What number should replace the question mark?
    AVIATOR = 6
    FIXTURE = 9
    WIZARDS = 1
    DIVERSE = ?

30. Find a six-letter word using only these four letters:
    L I W O.

31. Find the number to replace the question mark.
    0.67, 0.69, 0.48, 0.88, 0.29, 1.07, ?

32. Find the 10-letter word.
    _A_A_R_P_S

33. Fill in the blanks to find two words that are synonyms.

 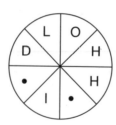

34.

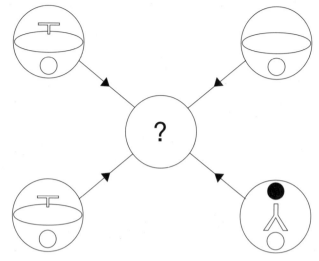

Each line and symbol that appears in the four outer circles, above, is transferred to the centre circle according to these rules. If a line or symbol occurs in the outer circles:

once: it is transferred
twice: it is possibly transferred
3 times: it is transferred
4 times: it is not transferred

Which of the circles A, B, C, D or E, shown below, should appear at the centre of the diagram, above?

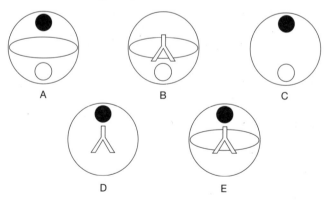

35. What activity is langlauf?

    a. boating
    b. fishing
    c. skating
    d. skiing

36. What number should replace the question mark?

71	63	4	2	19
32	8	16	25	34
9	12	43	61	7
4	35	26	18	?

37.

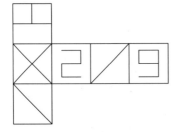

When the above is folded to form a cube, which is the only one of the following that *cannot* be produced?

A   B   C

D   E

38. What country is missing from the brackets as in the example?

blade (Bangladesh) gnash

lover (_ _ _ _ _ _ _ _ _) salad

39. Move in any direction to find a 10-letter word; each letter must only be used once.

Z	D	S	L	H
X	J	O	P	W
E	Y	M	R	F
C	I	G	T	U
V	N	A	K	B

40. What number should replace the question mark?

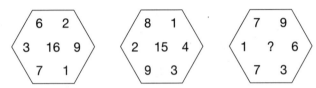

Questions

1.

Which option continues the above sequence?

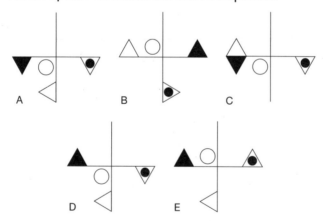

2. A bag of potatoes weighs 16 kg divided by a quarter of its weight. How much does the bag weigh?

3. Rift is to valley as mesa is to:

desert, mountain, plain, hill, highland

4. Which two words are most opposite in meaning?

inbound, intricate, erratic, warm, simple, fertile

5. Transfer the squares into the blank grid in such a way that a two-letter word is formed by each pair of adjoining letters and a 12-letter word is formed reading clockwise around the outside perimeter.

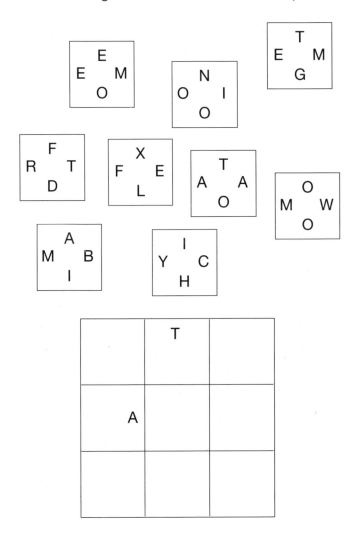

6. Which is the odd one out?

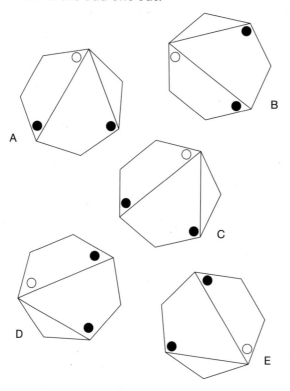

7. If planet A takes two years to revolve once round its sun, and planet B takes one year, when will they next both be in line with the sun?

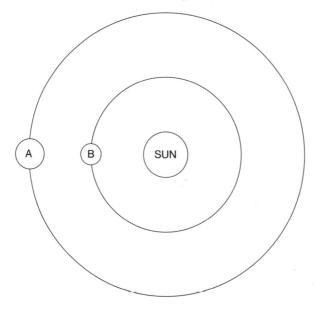

8. A well-known phrase has been divided into groups of three letters, which have then been placed in the wrong order. Find the phrase.

EBU EHO ETH LLB RNS TAK YTH

9.

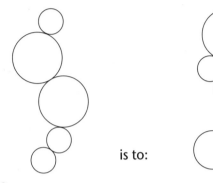

is to:

as

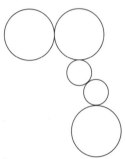

is to:

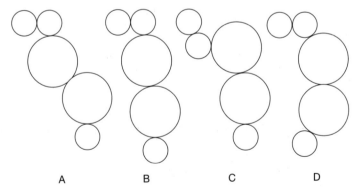

    A   B   C   D

10. What letter is missing from the centre?

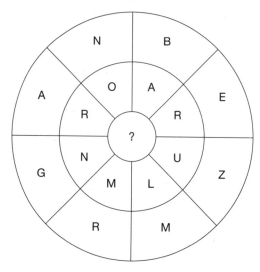

11. What number should replace the question mark?

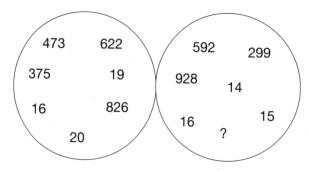

12. The name of which Shakespearean character can be inserted into the bottom line in order to complete nine three-letter words reading downwards?

M	A	W	H	H	H	W	B	S
I	C	A	A	U	I	H	A	E
_	_	_	_	_	_	_	_	_

13.

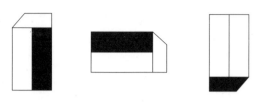

What comes next in the above sequence?

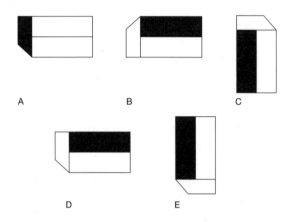

A   B   C

D   E

14. Change one letter only from each word to form a well-known phrase.

AS SHE READS

15. Solve this one-word anagram.

BARGAIN OIL

16. What number should replace the question mark?

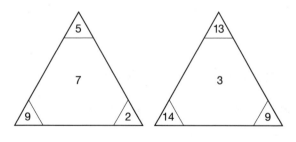

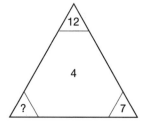

17. Use each letter of the newspaper headline below once each only to
spell out the names of three types of fruit.

No! An Amenable Groan

18. Insert the letters to find two words that form a phrase.

W L N I S T A T E C N D

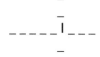

_ _ _ _ _ I _ _ _

Clue: peas in a pod.

19. If meat in a river (3 in 6) is T(ham)es, can you find a monkey in church
(3 in 6)?

20. Find the starting point and track from letter to adjacent letter horizontally and vertically, but not diagonally, to spell out a 12-letter word.
You have to provide the missing letters.

_	S	Y	_
T	_	A	O
A	S	C	_

21. Place the same four-letter word in front of these words to make new
words.

_ _ _ _ HOPPER
_ _ _ _ LET
_ _ _ _ BUD
_ _ _ _ LIKE
_ _ _ _ AGE

22. Find a one-word anagram for TORE GASH.

23. What number should replace the question mark?

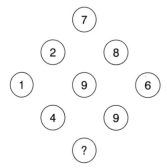

24. What weight should be placed at ? to make the scale balance?

6 kg   4 kg   ?   5 kg

25. Find a 10-letter word by moving from circle to circle; you may only use each circle once.

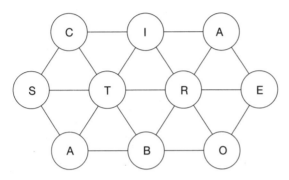

26. Fill in the blanks to find two words that are synonyms.

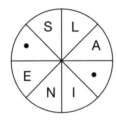 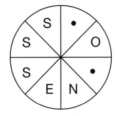

27.

Which circle should replace the question mark?

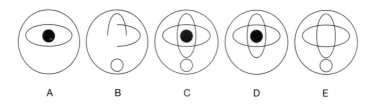

A   B   C   D   E

28. Which is the odd one out?

   a. hexagon
   b. pyramid
   c. square
   d. pentagon

29. Place two four-letter bits together to make an eight-letter word.

   AMPO ALIS LURE DENT TANT GREN SELE DEVO IRRI DINE

30. What is a drogger?

   a. castle
   b. boat
   c. caravan
   d. druggist

31. What is the next number in this series?

    −3, +6, +2, −3, +7, −12, ?

32.

12	9	14	10
15	34	5	11
7	4	3	23
26	13	16	18

In the arrangement of numbers above, what is the difference between the sum of the two highest odd numbers and the product of the two lowest even numbers?

33. Fill in the blanks to find two words that are antonyms.

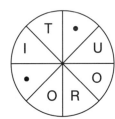 

34.

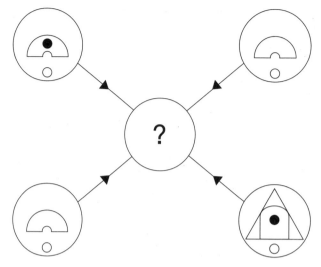

Each line and symbol that appears in the four outer circles, above, is transferred to the centre circle according to these rules. If a line or symbol occurs in the outer circles:

once: it is transferred
twice: it is possibly transferred
3 times: it is transferred
4 times: it is not transferred

Which of the circles A, B, C, D or E, shown below, should appear at the centre of the diagram, above?

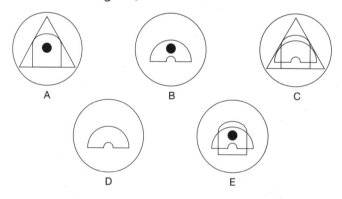

35. Which of the following is always part of comfit?

    a. peppercorns
    b. bacon
    c. ham
    d. sugar

36. Place two three-letter bits together to make a six-letter word.

    SPI, TLE, BUB, ANT, WOR, DAR, MIN, BEE, WAS, LER

    Clue: insect.

37. Which of these is not found in the kitchen?

    CUGPEG

    CIJRUE

    RAGRET

    DIGBRE

    LACSSE

38. Fill in the missing vowels to make a trite saying.

    TRSTV RYBDY BTLWY SCTTH CRDS

39. What word is indicated below?

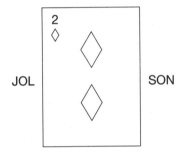

JOL   SON

40. Fill in the blanks to find a word.

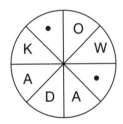

Questions

1. What numbers should replace the question marks?

2	6	30	?
3	5	11	?

2. Which is the odd one out?

   incumbent, obligatory, intrinsic, imperative, irremissible

3. What number should replace the question mark?

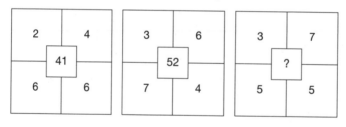

4. Which is the odd one out?

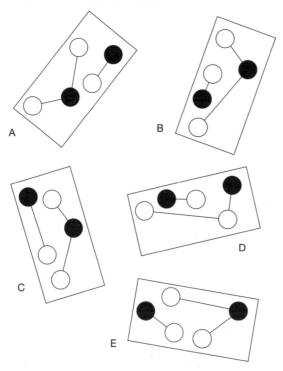

5. Newton is to force as kelvin is to:

frequency, pressure, light, temperature, sound

6. WRY SARAH is an anagram of which two words that are opposite in meaning?

7. Which word in brackets is closest in meaning to the word in capitals?

ERSTWHILE (notable, incorrect, near, cultured, past)

8. Start at one of the corner letters and spiral clockwise round the perimeter, finishing at the middle letter, to spell out a nine-letter word. You have to provide the missing letters.

```
_    N    O
T    E    _
R    O    P
```

9. Only one of the following groups of five letters can be arranged to form an English five-letter word. Can you find the word?

MERDO
HYOAL
NFOLE
HURSN
MUDAP

10. Insert the following words into the grid below:

ADROIT   ALAS   TAP
DEMAND   ASIA   ASK
                DESK   ADO
                BIND   ADD
                CHOP   MUD
                ROLE   ACT

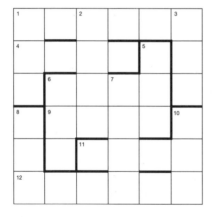

11.

Which square below has most in common with the square above?

A   B   C   D   E

12. What number should replace the question mark in the bottom right-hand triangle?

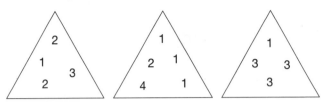

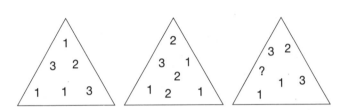

13. Insert two letters in each bracket so that they finish the word on the left and start the word on the right. The letters, when read downwards in pairs, will spell out an eight-letter word.

TA(_ _)IP
DU(_ _)SE
DI(_ _)CH
SO(_ _)LY

14. Which word is the odd one out?

carried
foolish
scarlet
quarter
mansion
fishing

15. Solve this one-word anagram:

STAR COUPLE

16.

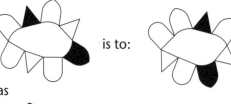

as

is to:

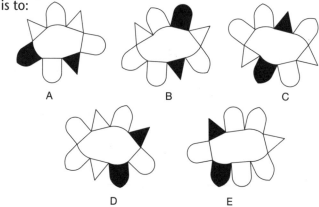

17. Which two letters should replace the question marks?

| A | W | F | N | ? |
| Z | C | S | J | ? |

18. Which is the odd one out?

RE500
50I1000E
NA5Y
TA101
GO50500
B50UE

19. What number should replace the question mark?

492, 366, 189, 810, ?

20.

What comes next in the above sequence?

A    D

B    E

C   F

21. What is a cairn?

    a. a loch
    b. a valley
    c. a heap of stones
    d. an outlook post

22. What have all these words in common?

    bartered
    timepiece
    patrician
    donated
    alfresco

23.

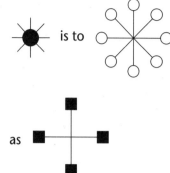

as

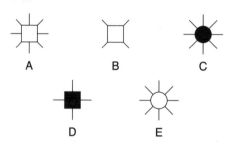

is to

A   B   C

D   E

24. Change one letter in each word to get three words that are members of the same category. For example, foul, sax, tin = four, six, ten.

weed, dab, near

25. What number should replace the question mark?

8	2	5	38
7	4	9	59
6	3	7	39
5	1	7	?

26. Fill in the blanks to find two words that are synonyms.

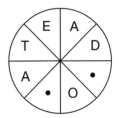 

27.

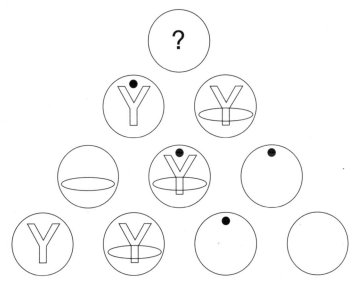

Which circle below should replace the question mark?

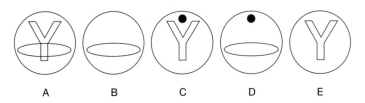

   A   B   C   D   E

28. Which of the following is not a cloud?

   a. cumulus
   b. stratus
   c. fumerole
   d. nimbus

29. Add vowels to make a trite saying.

    LLWRK NDNPL YMNSY MKMNY HNDVR FST

30. Find a six-letter word using only these four letters: W O N I

31. What is a fogle?
    a. musical instrument
    b. silk handkerchief
    c. hat
    d. shoes

32. What familiar phrase is suggested below?

    AS TAT EOF

33. Find the missing number.

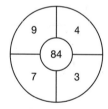 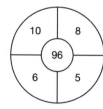 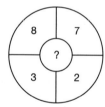

34.

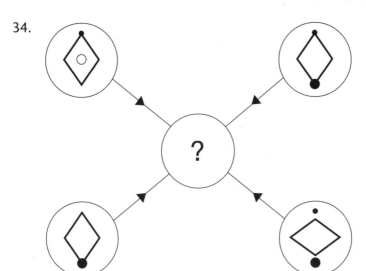

Each line and symbol that appears in the four outer circles, above, is transferred to the centre circle according to these rules. If a line or symbol occurs in the outer circles:

once: it is transferred
twice: it is possibly transferred
3 times: it is transferred
4 times: it is not transferred

Which of the circles A, B, C, D or E, shown below, should appear at the centre of the diagram, above?

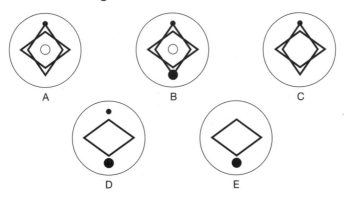

35. Which of the following is not an insect?
    GIAWER
    BASRAC
    SETEST
    RUBLEO
    THENOR

36. Find the missing number.
    $^7/_8$, $1^3/_8$, ?, $2^3/_8$, $2^7/_8$

37. Place two three-letter bits together to make a six-letter word.
    LIA PAN FOD DAH AST SIE DAF TUL IPE ERR
    Clue: flower.

38. Insert a word that means the same as the words outside the brackets.
    BOUNDARY (_ _ _ _) LAKE

39. Place the numbers 11 to 25 in the square so that each horizontal line, vertical line and the two diagonal lines all add up to 65.

	6		8	
			9	5
	7	1		
3				2
10			4	

40. Find the 10-letter word.
    _R_D_I_G_Y

1.

What comes next in the above sequence?

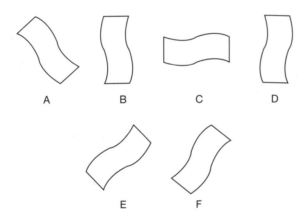

2. How many minutes is it before 12 noon if 20 minutes ago it was three times as many minutes after 9 am?

3. Which word in brackets is closest in meaning to the word in capitals?

GLUTINOUS (sad, cohesive, voracious, hungry, flushed)

4. INSECURE PET is an anagram of which two words that are opposite in meaning?

5.

Which option below continues the above sequence?

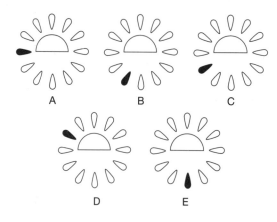

6. Which is the odd one out?

   nylon, vicuna, acrylic, polyester, acetate

7. Which two words that sound alike but are spelt differently, mean: essence, individual?

8. Which two rhyming words mean: trading residence?

9.

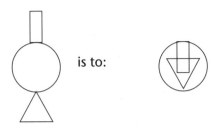

as

is to:

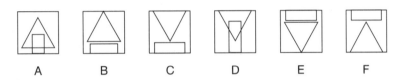

A   B   C   D   E   F

10. What number should replace the question mark?

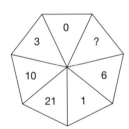

11. A well-known phrase has been divided up into groups of three letters, which have then been placed in the wrong order. Find the phrase.

ATO, EAC, INR, LIK, NAH, OOF, OTT

12. Start at one of the corner letters and spiral clockwise round the perimeter, finishing at the centre letter, to spell out a nine-letter word. You must provide the missing letters.

A   _   E
R   E   _
O   P   A

13.

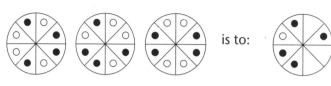

as

is to:

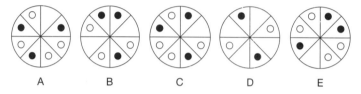

```
A        B        C        D        E
```

14. What is the longest English word that can be produced from the following 10 letters?

IFTWENPAML

15. Which number is the odd one out?

681422
751217
941319
831114
391221
691524
791625

16. Use every letter of the newspaper headline below, once each only, to spell out the names of three kinds of vegetable.

Chairperson Can Bat!

17. Which set of letters is the odd one out?

ADE
ILM
RUV
EHI
VYZ
JLM
FIJ

18.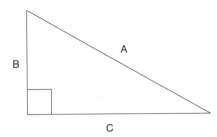

Pythagorean numbers occur when $a^2 = b^2 + c^2$, for example, $34^2 = 16^2 + 30^2$. Find another set of whole Pythagorean numbers where b also equals 16.

19. Complete the three words so that the same two letters that finish the first word start the second, the same two letters that finish the second word start the third and the same two letters that finish the third word also start the first word, thus completing the circle.

```
_ _ D U _ _
_ _ R E _ _
_ _ L U _ _
```

20. Insert two letters in each bracket so that they finish the word on the left and start the word on the right. The letters, when read downwards in pairs, will spell out an eight-letter word.

```
N A (_ _) S H
S A (_ _) S P
C A (_ _) E M
R E (_ _) C H
```

21. Which is the odd one out?

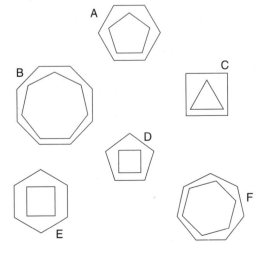

22. Find a one-word anagram for FLAT ROMP.

23. Find a six-letter word using only these four letters: L B U E.

24. What is a papillon?
    a. dog
    b. flower
    c. insect
    d. butterfly

25. What word is represented below?

26. Find a 10-letter word by moving from circle to circle; you may only use each circle once.

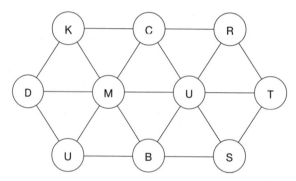

27. Each of the nine squares in the grid marked 1A to 3C should incorporate all the lines and symbols that are shown in the squares of the same letter and number immediately above and to the left. For example, 2B should incorporate all the lines and symbols that are in 2 and B.

    One of the squares is incorrect. Which one is it?

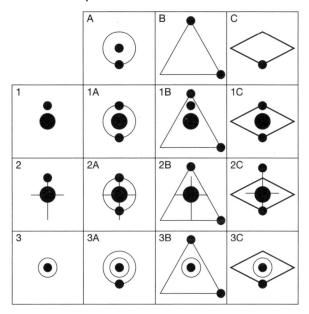

28. Place two four-letter bits together to equal an eight-letter word.

    ATES, SLIM, PARE, ORIC, COMP, OMEN, INGO,
    METE, ORIT, SENT

29. Place the same four-letter word in front of these words to make new words.

    _ _ _ _ WORK
    _ _ _ _ WARE
    _ _ _ _ ORE
    _ _ _ _ CLAD
    _ _ _ _ SMITH

30. Which of these is not a material?

    HARIMO
    TUBRET
    NETEAS
    SKAMAD
    LICOCA

31. Solve this code to find a saying.

    H JMZPS UCAIV XCPRN PALCM OQZVS UCCLV XTAIN PLACQ SMAPJ LSSAM

    Hint: the answer is unseen, but not much chance of it being OK!

32. Which circle cannot be made into a six-letter word?

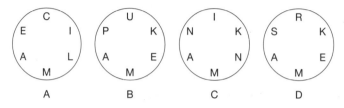

33. Fill in the blanks to find two words that are synonyms.

 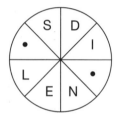

34.

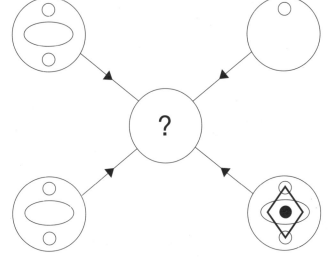

Each line and symbol that appears in the four outer circles, above, is transferred to the centre circle according to these rules. If a line or symbol occurs in the outer circles:

once: it is transferred
twice: it is possibly transferred
3 times: it is transferred
4 times: it is not transferred

Which of the circles A, B, C, D or E, shown below, should appear at the centre of the diagram, above?

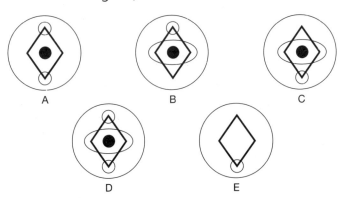

35. Which word is the opposite of pellucid?

    a. fragile
    b. clean
    c. opaque
    d. broken

36. Which two words mean the same?

    surprise, anger, felicity, benevolent, desire, bliss, delicate, stormy

37. All of the vowels have been removed from this trite saying. This is 'Cole's law'.

    THNLY SLCDC BBG

38. What is a melange?
    a. card game
    b. mixture
    c. caramel
    d. ice cream

39. Fill in the blanks and find two words that are synonyms.

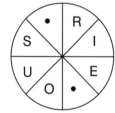 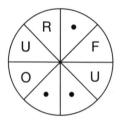

40. What familiar foodstuff is indicated below?

    CROISSA

Answers and explanations

Test 1: Answers

1. B;

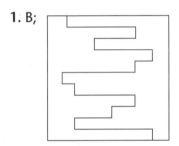

2. allow;   **3.** 20: add 1, 1, 2, 2, 3, 3, 4, 4;   **4.** 3527: in the others the sum of the first two numbers is equal to the sum of the second two numbers, for example 5 + 2 = 6 + 1;   **5.** pressure;   **6.** D: lines across proceed +1, +2, +3. Lines down proceed +3, +2, +1;   **7.** C: in all the others the black circle is connected to three white circles. In C it is only connected to two white circles;   **8.** weight, speed;

9.

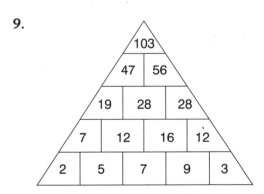

10. B: the rest are the same figure rotated;   **11.** 44 minutes: 12 noon less 44 minutes = 11.16, 11.16 less 48 minutes = 10.28, 9 am plus 88 minutes (44 × 2) = 10.28;   **12.** SHIVER, EROTIC, ICICLE, LENGTH, THRASH;   **13.** cube: it is a three-dimensional figure. The rest are all two-dimensional figures;   **14.** Switch A is faulty;   **15.** B: in each line and column, each of the three rings is shaded black once;   **16.** impact;   **17.** WIN BOAR = rainbow. The foods are spaghetti (PAST EIGHT), macaroni (I CAN ROAM), pancake (CAN PEAK) and chocolate (COOL CHEAT);   **18.** 4: looking across at the three circles, the number in the middle is the product of the two numbers in the same segment in the other two circles. Thus, 3 × 2 = 6, 7 × 3 = 21 and 4 × 4 = 16;   **19.** PROFESSIONAL;   **20.** 11;   **21.** D: in each line across and down the arrows point in each of three directions left, right and down. The number of arrows increases 1, 2, 3 in each row;   **22.** $5\frac{1}{16}$: there are two alternate sequences: $-1\frac{1}{4}$ and $+1\frac{1}{4}$;   **23.** linguist, polyglot;   **24.** 888, 890: the sequence progresses ×3, +2;   **25.** take: all words can be prefixed with PAR to form another word – parable, parrot, parson, parking, partake;   **26.** swimmer, skier;   **27.** place/pace;   **28.** Alf 144, Jim 36, Sid 12;   **29.** sexed Utah = exhausted. The words meaning out of this world are: wonderful (flow under), unbelievable (enviable blue), incredible (icier blend);   **30.** 40 socks. If he takes out 38 socks, although it is very unlikely, it is possible they could all be blue and red. To make 100 per cent certain that he also has a pair of black socks he must take out a further two socks;

31.

The black dot is moving up (then down) by one position at each stage;

32. 37 minutes: 12 noon less 37 minutes = 11.23, 11.23 less nine minutes = 11.14.10 am plus 74 minutes (2 × 37) = 11.14;   **33.** medley, conglomeration;   **34.** evil: when joined together each pair of words forms another word – brokerage, prosecute, daredevil;   **35.** 93541;   **36.** D: so that one dot appears in the triangle and one circle; and the other dot appears in the triangle and three circles;   **37.** HANG GLIDER;   **38.** G;   **39.** 0: looking at lines of numbers from the top: 9 × 8 = 72; 72 × 8 = 576; 576 × 8 = 4608;   **40.** C: each opposite corner block of four squares are identical.

Test 2: Answers

1. E: the number of white dots is increased by one each time, both vertically and horizontally, and all white dots are connected;   **2.** PART: RAMPART and PARTRIDGE;   **3.** B: lines across proceed +2, –3, +2. Lines down proceed –3, +2, –3;   **4.** glass;   **5.** 5: (8 + 7) × 5 = 75;   **6.** fact is stranger than fiction; **7.** B: black objects turn to white and vice versa;   **8.** 7.5: the sequence proceeds +4, ÷2, +4, etc;   **9.** meridian, parallel;   **10.** B: in lines and columns, add the first three numbers to arrive at the fourth number;   **11.** observe;

12.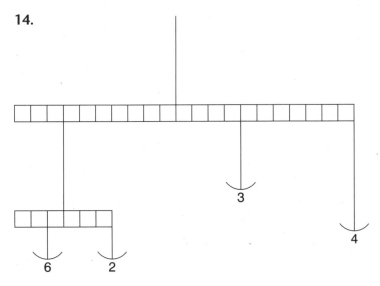

Tile 7 is incorrect, and should be replaced by tile B;

13. frivolity, sobriety;

14.

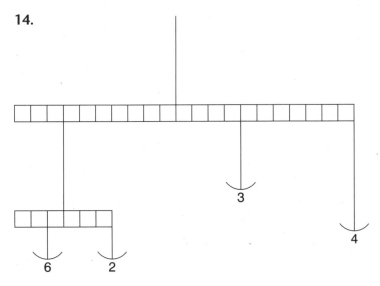

$6 \times 1 = 2 \times 3$: $7 \times 8 (6 + 2) = 56$, $11 \times 4 = 44$, $4 \times 3 = 12$, $44 + 12 = 56$;

15. weigh hay;   **16.** D;   **17.** mandible: it is the jaw bone, the rest are bones in the leg;   **18.** 10 pm: 12 noon = 12 noon, 1 pm = 12.43, 2 pm = 1.26, 3 pm = 2.09, 4 pm = 2.52,+6 hours = 10 pm;   **19.** OPTICAL ILLUSION;   **20.** A: each line across and down contains five black dots and four white dots;   **21.** A: the figure is tumbling 45° at each stage and alternates white/black/striped;   **22.** crossfire: all words contain an embedded tree – do(pine)ss, uncl(oak)ing, dishw(ash)er, cross(fir)e;   **23.** 57: there are two alternate sequences: +14, –97;   **24.** C;   **25.** 27, 9, 12: the sequence progresses ÷3, +3, ×3, –3 repeated;   **26.** D: it contains a triangle in a circle, a circle in a triangle (with the same orientation of the triangle) and a black dot in a square;   **27.** minimum;   **28.** 7: 91 ÷ 13;   **29.** Switch D is faulty;   **30.** coalesce;   **31.** 17: it is the sum of the two digits (9 + 8) in the quadrant directly opposite;   **32.** E: so that the dot appears in two circles and the square;   **33.** 32: the next cube number below 64 (4 × 4 × 4) is 27 (3 × 3 × 3). In order to construct a solid cube, therefore, with none left over, 59 – 27 = 32 blocks need to be taken away;   **34.** DERIVE/DRIVE;   **35.** 49: (73 + 25) ÷ 2;   **36.** COMPUTE;   **37.** D: the last two rows of figures repeat the first two rows of figures in reverse;   **38.** MEDIOCRE, SUPERIOR;   **39.** 8: each number in the segment at the bottom is the sum of the four numbers in the sections either side. Thus: 8 + 3 + 4 + 3 = 18;   **40.** E.

Test 3: Answers

1. E: only lines that appear three times in the same position in the first three squares are carried forward to the final square;   **2.** trombone: the rest are percussion instruments;   **3.** head of school = principal, fundamental truth = principle, standing still = stationary, writing materials = stationery, smaller in amount = less, smaller in number = fewer (score 1 point if all answers are correct);   **4.** 683: in the other numbers add the first and last digits to arrive at the middle digit;   **5.** PAST, FUTURE;   **6.** L;   **7.** D: to each arc, add a quarter of a circle clockwise;   **8.** ESCALATE, HEIGHTEN;   **9.** 30, 26: there are two alternate sequences. Add 5 starting at 1. Subtract 5 starting at 50;   **10.** acellular, acerbated, acerbates, acescence, acescency, acetabula, acetamide, acetified;   **11.** D;   **12.** B: start at the bottom left-hand corner square and work along the bottom row, then back along the next row up etc, repeating the numbers 38219;   **13.** government;   **14.** E: each line across and down contains one each of the three symbols. In each line one symbol is black, and one is upside down;   **15.** PAMPHLET, BROCHURE;

16. VHU: the numbers spelled out below are the number of sides in the figures in which they appear;

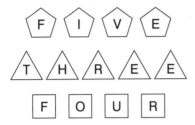

17. 4: 6 × 9 = 54 (reading down the middle two blocks);   **18.** quirky;   **19.** 600: 72 ÷ 12 × 100;   **20.** C: looking across and down the triangles turn through 90°;   **21.** IVH: the first letter moves three places in the alphabet forwards: Fghl; the second letter moves four letters in the alphabet forwards: RstuV; the third letter moves two places in the alphabet backwards: JiH;   **22.** C;   **23.** C: each circle is repeated rotated;   **24.** PROPELLER;   **25.** 11: there are two alternate sequences: +3 and –4;

26. $\dfrac{14}{55} \times \dfrac{77}{56} = \dfrac{1}{5} \times \dfrac{7}{4} = \dfrac{7}{20}$

27. C: each row and column contains six complete lines and six broken lines;   **28.** improbable;   **29.** £8.00 per person: starter = 1 unit, sweet = 2 units, main course = 4 units, = 7 units in total. Therefore, cost per unit = £56 ÷ 7 = £8.00. The main course, therefore, cost 4 × 8 = 32 (or £8.00 per person);   **30.** maroon: the letters start and finish with the alphabetic sequence: ABcDEfGHiJKlMN;   **31.** C: the top arm moves 45° clockwise at each stage and the bottom arm moves 90° clockwise;   **32.** 55: each number indicates its position in the grid. 55 indicates row 5 column 5;   **33.** GET A MOVE ON;   **34.** B: only dots that appear in the same position just twice in the first three hexagons are carried forward to the final hexagons;   **35.** 12: add the digits of each three-figure number to obtain the two-digit numbers;   **36.** NO STRINGS ATTACHED;   **37.** C: in each row and column only lines that are common to the first two squares are carried forward to the final square;   **38.** They will never appear together in the same corner as in a heptagon three corners clockwise is the same as four corners anticlockwise;   **39.** CHAMELEON: to produce ARC, ASH, SEA, GEM, PIE, AIL, HUE, AGO, MAN;

40.

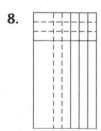

| 5 | 18 |
| 36 | 15 |

Top left is a third of bottom right, bottom right is three less than top right and top right is half of bottom left.

Test 4: Answers

1. B: the inner hexagon is being dismantled one side at a time working anti-clockwise, while the outer hexagon is being constructed one side at a time working clockwise;   **2.** 92.2: deduct 2.6 at each stage;   **3.** DISAPPEAR;
4. 3649: in all the others multiply the first two digits together to produce the number formed by the last two digits;   **5.** practicable, feasible;
6. second, last;   **7.** 72932;

8.

Vertical lines turn dotted, one at a time at each stage. One horizontal line is added at each stage, and the previous lines become dotted;

9. dishevelled;   **10.** 1417: 42 ÷ 3 = 14, 51 ÷ 3 = 17;   **11.** ADD FUEL TO THE FIRE;   **12.** E: the rest are the same figure rotated;   **13.** tributary: in the other words the prefix tri- refers to three;   **14.** 7: the numbers round the centre increase by seven (in the others they increase by three and five respectively);   **15.** 157: 7 + 8 = 15, 2 + 5 = 7;   **16.** B: looking across an outer circle is removed, looking down an outer circle is added;   **17.** silk;
18. 425136 or 631524;   **19.** SKYSCR(APE)R;   **20.** D: looking across, the dot in the top left-hand quarter moves to the opposite corner, the dot in the top right-hand quarter moves one corner anticlockwise at each stage, the dot in the bottom left-hand quarter moves between the top two corners, and the dot in the bottom right-hand quarter moves one corner clockwise at each stage;   **21.** C: the first three arcs are being repeated; and the position of the arc shifts 180°;   **22.** EXPAND, REDUCE;   **23.** C: looking across each line add three; looking down each column add two;   **24.** chord, cord;

25. Mary 16, George 17, Alice 24, Stephen 56, Claire 71;   **26.** E: looking across and down, lines are carried forward from the first two squares to the final square when they appear in the same position twice in the first two squares. However, they then change from complete to broken lines, and vice versa;   **27.** ILLICIT;   **28.** 9: $(7 \times 9) \div (7 \times 1)$;   **29.** FOLLOWER, DISCIPLE;

30.

The white dot moves corner/side/corner anticlockwise and the black dot does the same clockwise;

31. elicit: the following word begins with the last two letters of the previous word reversed;   **32.** pentagon;   **33.** 9;   **34.** A: looking across the squares, the top left corner alternates one line/two lines/three lines; the top right corner alternates line right vertical/line left vertical; the bottom left corner alternates top horizontal/ bottom horizontal and the bottom right corner alternates diagonal between opposite corners;   **35.** 5/8 or 0.625 or 62.5 per cent;   **36.** F;   **37.** HIBERNATE;   **38.** 1: work backwards from 120; that is, $120 - 60 - 12 - 3 - 1$;   **39.** D: all lines are continued. However, wavy lines become straight and vice versa;   **40.** 52: start at the top left corner and work along the top line, then back along the second line, etc, adding nine then deducting three.

Test 5: Answers

1. C: it has three white and one black on the left and three black and one white on the right. The rest are the opposite way round;   **2.** cheeky;
3. ear, brain;   **4.** 6957: all the rest progress +3, –2, +3;   **5.** CIRCUMNAVI-GATION;   **6.** 12;   **7.** 150, 157: the sequence progresses +1, ×2, +3, ×4, +5, ×6, +7;   **8.** alleviate: it means to lessen, the rest meaning to increase;
9. 4: $(6 + 7) - (4 + 5)$;   **10.** OCTOPUS: to produce DUO, ARC, SAT, AGO, MAP, YOU, WAS;   **11.** C: at each stage the third circle moves to the end and the sixth circle moves to the beginning;   **12.** 8: the number in the middle is the average of the numbers round the outside. So, 7 + 8 + 9 + 7 + 8 + 9 = 48, and 48 ÷ 6 = 8;   **13.** MAGNETISM;   **14.** 115: in eight years the combined age is 124; the age now is $124 - (8 \times 3) = 100$. Age in five years is $100 + (5 \times 3) = 115$;   **15.** ripe, mellow;   **16.** C: all lines carry on and change from dotted to unbroken, and vice versa;
17. crevice;   **18.** Jack 10 and Jill 5;   **19.** COME TO LIFE;

20.

The sequence progresses circle, triangle, diamond, with alternate horizontal/ vertical lines;

21. 730: deduct 135 each time;   **22.** C: it contains four black dots and three white;   **23.** might/mite;   **24.** 2646 (14 × 189);   **25.** using few words;   **26.** SATURATE, WATERLOG;   **27.** 65: there are two alternate sequences: +12 and +9;   **28.** C: the large rectangle is being dismantled, half a side at a time anticlockwise; the small rectangle is being constructed half a side at a time clockwise;   **29.** TESTIMONY;   **30.** 6: so that the numbers in the triangles, squares and circles add up to 33;   **31.** C: so that one dot appears in one triangle and the other dot appears in two triangles (in the example the right-hand side forms a small triangle and a larger trian-gle and the dot is in both);   **32.** 9: the alternatives are: England win both golf and tennis, Scotland win both golf and tennis, Wales win both golf and tennis, England win golf, Scotland win tennis, Scotland win golf, England win tennis, England win golf, Wales win tennis, Wales win golf, England win tennis, Scotland win golf, Wales win tennis, Wales win golf, Scotland win tennis;   **33.** retirement: statement/testament and fluster/restful are anagram pairs;   **34.** Switch A is faulty;   **35.** 2: so that each square block of four numbers totals 15;   **36.** E: the small ellipse moves 45° clockwise and alternates inside/outside of the larger ellipse;   **37.** BARRIER REEF;   **38.** K; **39.** 3645: in all the others the number formed by the first two digits added to the number formed by the second two digits equals 99;   **40.** B: looking across and down, only dots that appear in the same position in the first two squares are carried forward to the third square; however, they then change from black to white and vice versa.

Test 6: Answers

1. OSCILLATE, FLUCTUATE;   **2.** 47: each number is the sum of the previous two numbers, ie 18 + 29 = 47;   **3.** expand, reduce;   **4.** E;   **5.** fry;   **6.** 40 minutes: (70 × 8) ÷ 14. Total time for eight players = 70 × 8 = 560 minutes. However, as 14 people are each on the pitch for an equal length of time, they are each on the pitch for 40 minutes (560 ÷ 14);   **7.** two sides to every story;

8.

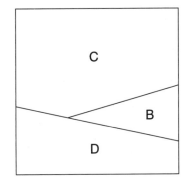

9. abutment: it is part of a structure, the rest are specific types of arch;
10. 4: in each row and column in order to arrive at the final number multiply the first two numbers together and divide by 6;   **11.** F;   **12.** D: looking both across and down, only lines that appear in both the first two squares are carried forward to the third square;   **13.** TO LIE IN WAIT;

14.

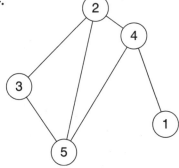

15. PANORAMIC;   **16.** C: only lines and symbols that appear just twice in the outer circles appear in the inner circle;   **17.** SUCCINCT, RAMBLING;
18. the Arctic = architect. The buildings are: cathedral (delta arch), minaret (raiment), castle (cleats), bungalow (a blowgun);   **19.** 40 days: five men take $5 \times 16 = 80$ man days to build the house. Two men will, therefore, take 40 days to build the house ($80 \div 2$);   **20.** A: each pair of circles are mirror images of each other;   **21.** E: the number of sides reduces by one at each stage, and the section two clockwise from the single white dot disappears;
22. come to life;   **23.** MOP. JklM – RqpO – MnoP;   **24.** 11615: $8 + 3 = 11$;
$1 + 5 = 6$; $9 + 6 = 15$;   **25.** FREE, LIBERATE;   **26.** C: the two circles overlap each other and the square; the triangle and square overlap;
27. rues/ruse;

28. $\dfrac{27}{74} \times \dfrac{37}{9} \times \dfrac{6}{17} = \dfrac{3}{2} \times \dfrac{6}{17} = \dfrac{18}{34} = \dfrac{9}{17}$

29. N;

30.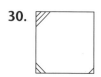

At each stage lines are added to a new corner working anticlockwise and a new line is added to corners already containing a line;

31. 6: 36 × 2 = 72; 14 × 2 = 28 and 43 × 2 = 86;   **32.** hold: to form compound words: nightlong, longboat, boathouse, household;   **33.** sword;   **34.** 32: 6 × 4 = 6 + 18, 7 × 3 = 11 + 10, 9 × 2 = 5 + 13, 16 × 4 = 32 + 32;   **35.** B: looking across and down add another circle, alternating black/white, to alternate squares;   **36.** 1: average 45 ÷ 9= 5; second lowest even number = 4;   **37.** 2 kilograms: half weight = 1 kg (+1 kg) = 2 kg;   **38.** EUCALYPTUS, SANDALWOOD;   **39.** 5: (6 + 8) – 9;   **40.** B: so that each connected straight line of three circles contains one each of the three different types of star.

Test 7: Answers

1. A: the square goes inside the diamond and the diamond in turn goes inside the pentagon, which turns onto its base;   **2.** staff: it is a support for a flag. The rest are all types of flag;   **3.** £900: change everything to twentieths. So, $^8/_{20}$ + $^{11}/_{20}$ = $^{19}/_{20}$. Therefore, £45.00 must be equal to $^1/_{20}$ and the original sum of money must be 45 × 20 = 900;**4.** C;   **5.** elemental;   **6.** WIND: HEADWIND and WINDLASS;   **7.** 1: the number formed at the top is half of the number formed at the bottom, ie 358 × 2 = 716;

8.

5	3	7
8	6	2
1	9	4

The above numbers indicate the order in which the nine squares should be visited from the starting point (the square numbered 1) through to the finishing point (the treasure square number 9);

9. B: looking across, the dot moves 45° clockwise at each stage, but looking down it moves 45° anticlockwise;   **10.** A: lines across progress, in turn, –1, –3, –5, –4;   **11.** proficient, unskilled;   **12.** venture, introduce;   **13.** 971613: numbers are obtained by adding pairs of digits, ie with 571219: 5 + 7 = 12; 7 + 12 = 19. To follow this same pattern 971613 would have to be 971623;   **14.** pull wool;   **15.** B: the dot moves corner/side anticlockwise, the straight line and the curved line both move corner to corner clockwise;   **16.** 72.5: the amount deducted increases by 2.75 each time, ie 2.75, 5.5, 8.25, 11;   **17.** tree;   **18.** 32: the total of three numbers must be 48 × 3 = 144. The total of two numbers must be 56 × 2 = 112. Therefore, 144 – 112 = 32;   **19.** actions speak louder than words;   **20.** 6;   **21.** OBLIGATE;   **22.** PUSH THE BOAT OUT;   **23.** E: the rectangle starting on the left is moving from left to right one place at a time at each stage;   **24.** 83: there are two alternate sequences: +3 and –4;   **25.** stead: to give homestead and steadfast;

26.

5	2	8	6
6	5	9	1
3	6	3	9
7	8	1	5

27. DORMOUSE and SQUIRREL;   **28.** F: looking across and down, lines are carried forward from the first two squares to the final square, except where two lines appear in the same position in the first two squares, in which case they are cancelled out;   **29.** EVIDENTIAL;   **30.** 9: (6 + 17) – (5 + 9);   **31.** B: the white dots are each moving left to right and bottom to top (and vice versa) one place at a time at each stage;   **32.** D;   **33.** 82: combined age in 9 years time will be 94 – (3 × (13 – 9));   **34.** ASSEMBLE, DISPERSE;   **35.** 31 and 4: 12 × 7 = 84; 8 + 12 + 7 + 4 = 31;   **36.** B: the left side contains the same symbols as the right side but with black/white reversal;   **37.** Switch B is faulty;   **38.** PALATABLE, TASTELESS;   **39.** 6: 5749827 + 3864759 = 9614586;   **40.** E: looking across and down, lines are carried forward from the first two squares to the final square, except where two lines appear in the same position in the first two squares, in which case they are cancelled out.

Test 8: Answers

1. 19, 21, 24: the sequence progresses +1, +2, +3 repeated;   **2.** crater/cater;
3. 8;   **4.** B: looking across, the letters jump +2, +3 in the alphabet, for example – AbCdeF. Looking down, they progress +4, +5, for example – AbcdEfghiJ;   **5.** D: so the dot appears in the diamond and circle only;   **6.** PUPILS SLIP UP;   **7.** 2 6, 0 3. Looking across, the numbers in the same position in each pair progress: 8, 6, 4, 2; 3, 4, 5, 6; 9, 6, 3, 0; 6, 5, 4, 3;

8.

The top left-hand corner alternates black dot/white dot; the top right-hand corner alternates horizontal line/vertical line; the bottom left-hand corner line moves diagonal/vertical/diagonal/horizontal/diagonal, and the bottom right-hand corner alternates white dot/black dot;

9. sow: it is a female animal, the rest are male;   **10.** Margaret 17, Stuart 12, Jeffrey 32, Brian 25 and Philip 21;   **11.** CREATIVITY, REACTIVITY;

12.

Tile 6 is incorrect and should be replaced by tile E;

13. watertight, tenuous;   **14.** 6: the total of the numbers in each column alternates 20, 30, 20, 30, 20, 30;   **15.** GESTURE;   **16.** A;   **17.** overt;   **18.** Harry 32, Larry 24, Carrie 18;   **19.** salubrious, healthy;   **20.** F: the circle becomes a square and the four white squares become white circles;   **21.** D: looking across, the number of dots increases by one and white becomes black. Looking down, the number of dots decreases by one and the dots stay the same colour;   **22.** ABSOLUTE MAJORITY;   **23.** Switch C is faulty;   **24.** C: the black square originally in the top right-hand corner is moving right to left one space at a time at each stage. The other black square is moving from bottom to top;   **25.** LINE OF WORK;   **26.** 1456 (91 × 16);   **27.** ANOIP = PIANO;   **28.** 12.25: add 1.25, 1.5, 1.75, 2, 2.25, 2.5;   **29.** hand: second hand, handsome;   **30.** E: looking across, the number of lines increases. Looking down, the number of circles increases by one and the circles fit within the bands formed by the lines;   **31.** 22 minutes. Midnight less 22 minutes = 11.38. Less 32 minutes = 11.06. 10 pm (22.00) plus 66 minutes (22 × 3) = 11.06;   **32.** tiara. The consonants b t r n and l are being repeated in the same order;   **33.** LENGTHEN, DIMINISH;   **34.** 131: add 30, 28, 26, 24, 22;

35.

The large circle moves 45° clockwise and alternates white/black. The centre dot alternates black/white;

36. LAND LOCKED;   **37.** DISBELIEF;

38. $\dfrac{5}{9} \times \dfrac{18}{15} = \dfrac{2}{3}$

39. 50 per cent: it is a certainty that at least two coins will land with the same side face up. It is equally likely that these two coins will land heads up as they will land tails upwards. It is immaterial what occurred in the previous toss;   **40.** B: it has three circles of differing sizes, one triangle, one dot out on its own, one dot in the large circle only and the other dot in the middle-sized circle and triangle.

Test 9: Answers

1. A: square 1 moves to bottom right, square 2 moves to top left, square 3 moves to top right and square 4 moves to bottom left;   **2.** HIDE, REVEAL;   **3.** black, olive, fawn, cyan, pink;   **4.** A: lines across progress +2, +4, +6, + 8 in turn. Columns down progress +3, +5, +7, +9 in turn;   **5.** D;   **6.** H: in all the others the outer figure is repeated in the middle;   **7.** TENDER LOVING CARE;   **8.** 2: the total of the numbers in the shaded section in each hexagon is half the total of the remaining numbers;   **9.** include: each word begins with the sixth and fifth letters of the preceding word;

10.

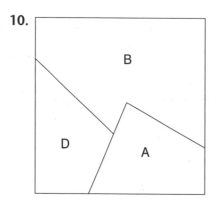

11. SCARE, ALARM;   **12.** pit;   **13.** 85647: reverse the first number and discard the highest and lowest digits;   **14.** U: AbCdeFghiJklmnOpqrstU;

15.

Tile 8 is incorrect and should be replaced by tile B;

16. 81: add 27 each time;   **17.** calypso: it is a song, the rest are dances;
18. B: looking across, lines progress +4, looking down, columns progress
+3;   **19.** Stella: each name begins with the middle two letters of the previous name;   **20.** C;   **21.** E: it contains exactly the same symbols as the original;   **22.** 4: all lines and columns total 18;   **23.** GERANIUM, DAFFODIL;
24. C: the contents of each pentagon are determined by the contents of the
two pentagons immediately below it. Lines and dots are carried forward
from these two pentagons, except when a line or dot appears in the same
position, in which case they are cancelled out;   **25.** PEACH, OLIVE,
COCONUT;   **26.** 13: opposite numbers total 15;

27.

Lines are added vertically then horizontally alternately;

28. HARMFUL, SAFE;   **29.** 1394: (82 × 17);   **30.** reef: acti(**on e**)ffor(**t
wo**)r(**th ree**) (**f our**)self;

31.

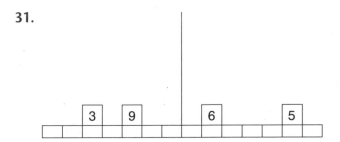

5 × 3 = 15, 3 × 9 = 27, 15 + 27 = 42, 30 + 12 = 42, 6 × 5 = 30, 2 × 6 = 12;

32. 5: each row of numbers contains the digits 1–9;   **33.** C: the arms move
clockwise in turn 45°;   **34.** water: to give salt water, waterfall;   **35.** detonator: the rest contain the letters 'der' adjacently;   **36.** £43.20: Christine = £24
or five parts, therefore, each part = £4.80. Total of nine parts shared = £4.80
× 9 = £43.20;   **37.** £54.00: Christine's share = £24.00 or four parts, therefore, each part = £6.00. Total of nine parts shared = £54.00;   **38.** D: the
diamond is moving round each corner clockwise. The black portion alternates overlapping section/diamond/square;   **39.** PRAISEWORTHY;

40. A B C D

7	9	4	5
13	11	14	9
25	27	20	23
47	45	50	43
95	97	88	93

The numbers in each row are determined, as follows, by the numbers in the row above: A + C = B; B + D = C; B + C = A; C + D = D.

Test 10: Answers

1. 17: 8 + 9 = 17; 7 + 6 = 13;   **2.** bland;   **3.** 86: the amount deducted increases by 0.5 each time, ie 0.5, 1, 1.5, 2, 2.5, 3, 3.5;   **4.** Switch B is not working;   **5.** D: so that the dot is in the square and two circles;   **6.** deltoid: it means triangular in shape. The rest mean double or twofold;   **7.** 2: in rows and columns alternate digits total the same, for example 5 + 9 = 10 + 4;   **8.** METEORIC: to give some/melt, late/test, door/oral, epic/icon;   **9.** C: the rest are the same figure rotated;   **10.** The fathers' rights activist's dog buried its bone in the garden;   **11.** 6394: all the others are in pairs where the second and fourth digits change places: 5278/5872, 9416/9614, 7895/7598, 6231/6132;   **12.** D: the contents of each pentagon are determined by the contents of the two pentagons immediately below it. Only when a dot appears in one of the corner positions or centre just once in these two pentagons, is it carried forward to the pentagon above;   **13.** austere; **14.** EJBATC = ABJECT;   **15.** 6471589: reverse the first three digits, then the last four digits;   **16.** E: it contains a triangle in a circle, a circle in a square and a black dot in a triangle;   **17.** spur;

18.

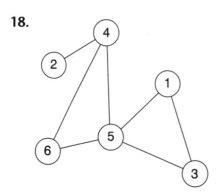

Alternatively as above but with 1 and 3 reversed;

19. BELL: BLUEBELL, BELLOWED;   **20.** C: in each row and column the contents of the third square is determined by the contents of the first two squares. Lines are transferred from these two squares to the third square, except when they appear in the same position in both squares, in which case they are cancelled out;   **21.** C: a line is added at the top and bottom alternately;   **22.** haughty, arrogant;   **23.** Switch B is faulty;   **24.** SPINACH, CARROT, POTATO;   **25.** B: the figure is tumbling over and alternates white/striped;   **26.** revival, extinction;   **27.** B;   **28.** irrational;   **29.** 25: there are two alternate sequences: +4 and −3;   **30.** cost: all the words have their letters in alphabetical order;   **31.** FRAME OF MIND;   **32.** D: the dot is in a triangle;   **33.** 5: 70 ÷ 14 = 5; 91 ÷ 13 = 7, 120 ÷ 24 = 5;   **34.** H;   **35.** PULL TO PIECES;   **36.** 46: start at 1 and work clockwise adding 3, 6, 9, 12, 15, 18;   **37.** D: so that it appears in a circle with three secants (lines) passing through it;   **38.** 425: (68 ÷ 16) × 100;

39. PAUSE:

    5 1   (1 2 3 4 5)   3 2   4
    E M P T Y (P R I S M) V I R U S
    D E P T H (P A U S E) D U A L S;

40. 13: the numbers in each circle total 100.

Test 11: Answers

1. E: divide into groups of four identical arrows. In each group of four, each arrow moves 90 degrees clockwise. One arrow appears black in each group moving forward one place each time;   **2.** INSULT, PRAISE;   **3.** COSMOPOLITAN;   **4.** 41 minutes;   **5.** F: the figure at the top of the main figure flips into it, and the figure originally inside flips out;   **6.** lupine: it is a word meaning wolf-like. The remaining words are all connected with foxes;   **7.** FLEET;

8.

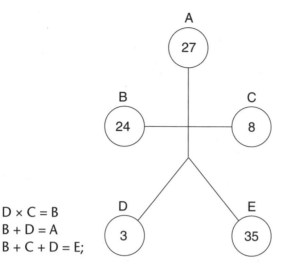

D × C = B
B + D = A
B + C + D = E;

9. C: looking down, a vertical line is added to the bell, and looking across, two horizontal lines are added;   **10.** colour: Beaufort is a scale of wind, Munsell is a scale of colours;   **11.** bawdiness (wise bands);

12. d. 87923

A	B	C	D	E		B	E	D	C	A
6	4	5	2	1		4	1	2	5	6
A	B	C	D	E		B	E	D	C	A
3	8	2	9	7		8	7	9	2	3;

13. 15;   **14.** GRACIOUS, MERCIFUL;   **15.** CHINA;   **16.** 239: 1 × 2 + 1 = 3; 3 × 3 + 2 = 11; 11 × 4 + 3 = 47; 47 × 5 + 4 = 239;   **17.** C: each segment is a mirror image of the segment opposite, but with black/white reversal; **18.** to hot up;   **19.** 72.5:the amount deducted increases by 2.75 each time, ie 2.75, 5.5, 8.25, 11;   **20.** F: all the others have an identical pairing; **21.** cats lie = elastic. The colours are: such tent = chestnut, cap riot = apricot, red navel = lavender, for fans = saffron;   **22.** D: the curl alternates left/right, the eyes alternate left/forward/right, the nose alternates black/white and the mouth alternates happy/sad/straight;

23. 17   10   15

12   14   16

13   18   11

Magic number 42;

24. D: A is the same as E but with black/white reversal, and similarly B is the same as C;   **25.** lope;   **26.** ALCOVE, VESSEL, ELAPSE, SERIAL;   **27.** 2 minutes 33 seconds (2.55 minutes). At 50 mph the train takes 2.125 × 60 ÷ 50 to pass through the tunnel, ie 2.55 minutes;   **28.** 16;   **29.** eat;   **30.** MONDAY;   **31.** 7 6 8 5 8. The first three lines are repeated, but reversed;   **32.** D: the rest are the same figure rotated;   **33.** PRO: PROFANE, PROPER;   **34.** TPHED = DEPTH;   **35.** 36: 32 ÷ 8 × 9 = 36. Similarly 12 ÷ 3 × 2 = 8 and 24 ÷ 6 × 7 = 28;   **36.** B: in all the others, only the portion common to all three figures is shaded;   **37.** b. to obscure;   **38.** TERMINAL VELOCITY;

39.

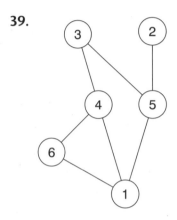

40. A: the contents of each hexagon are determined by the contents of the two hexagons directly below it. In the second row from the bottom, add the number of circles in the hexagons below. In the third row from the bottom take the difference ie, subtract, therefore, in the top circle add again, so one circle plus two circles means three circles in the top hexagon.

Test 12: Answers

1. D: first add one black dot to the horizontal, then two black dots to the vertical, then one white dot to the vertical and then two white dots to the horizontal;   **2.** SCENT, AROMA;   **3.** STEADFAST;   **4.** 4 mph. Say the journey is six miles each way. Then at 6 mph the outward jog would take one hour and the inward walk two hours. This means he takes three hours to travel 12 miles or one hour to travel four miles;   **5.** B: it contains one dot in one circle, one dot in two circles and one dot in three circles;   **6.** HAMPER;   **7.** 30 mph;   **8.** D: each horizontal and vertical line contains a circle, triangle and diamond. Also one square has no line, one has a vertical line and one a horizontal line;   **9.** indurate: this is a word meaning harden, the other words mean soften;   **10.** Shakespearean (a keen phrase as);   **11.**

verso, which is a word meaning a left-hand page and should, therefore, be in the left-hand column;   **12.** 5: the difference between 6 and 1 is 5, and the difference between 9 and 4 is 5. Similarly the difference between 7 and 3 is 4 and the difference between 5 and 2 is 3;   **13.** C: each fourth square contains a circle, each alternate square contains a diamond and each third square contains a dot;   **14.** superseded;   **15.** LIKE FATHER LIKE SON;   **16.** 9 pm;   **17.** C;   **18.** pet hens = Stephen. The buildings are: spoil hat = hospital, my bases = embassy, eel clog = college and admit us = stadium;   **19.** 9.25: add 1.65 each time;   **20.** D: the contents of each pentagon are determined by the contents of the two pentagons immediately below it. Lines are carried forward from these two pentagons, except when two lines appear in the same position, in which case they are cancelled out;   **21.** B: circles are only transferred to the middle circle when they appear in the same position just once in the four surrounding circles;   **22.** wizened, plump;   **23.** consternation (tennis cartoon);   **24.** 45: 36 ÷ 4 × 5; similarly 56 ÷ 8 × 5 = 35 and 42 ÷ 14 × 5 = 15;   **25.** D: each segment is moving 45 degrees clockwise at each stage;   **26.** cleverness;   **27.** FALL;   **28.** 7.5 kg: 9 × 5 = 45 and 6 × 7.5 = 45;   **29.** B: the rest are the same figure rotated;   **30.** year in year out;   **31.** 6: 58 − 49 = 9   3 × 18 = 54   54 ÷ 9 = 6;   **32.** B: the middle figure goes to the bottom, the right-hand figure goes to the top and rotates 180 degrees, the left-hand figure goes to the middle and rotates 180 degrees. The black dot goes to the top;   **33.** sabot: it is a shoe, the rest are hats;   **34.** dun;   **35.** 6: looking at the rows of numbers across, the totals from the top are 6, 7, 8, 9, 10;   **36.** D: A is the same as E with flaps in/out and similarly, B is the same as C;   **37.** ear;   **38.** bend over backwards;   **39.** 0: all numbers in the same position in each of the three squares add up to 10. Also, numbers formed in lines across add up to 1,110, eg, 574 + 212 + 324 = 1,110;   **40.** F: in each horizontal and vertical row of squares, the contents of the third square are determined by the contents of the first two squares. Lines are carried forward only when they appear in the same position in the first two squares.

Test 13: Answers

1.   BETRAYAL   DEVOTION;

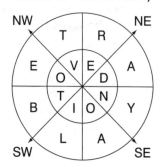

2. D: the rest are all the same figure rotated;   **3.** intricately (tiny article); **4.** 586: 69 + 517 = 586;   **5.** E: looking down, the line is moving 90 degrees anticlockwise and the white circle is moving 45 degrees clockwise. Looking across, the line is moving 45 degrees clockwise and the white circle is moving 90 degrees anticlockwise;   **6.** captivity;   **7.** STAMPEDE: to give MAST/STAR, TEAM/AMID, PIPE/PERT and TIDE/DEAL;   **8.** 237 yards: eight holes average 156 = 1,248 yards, nine holes average 162 = 1,458 yards (+ 210), nine holes average 165 = 1,485 yards (+ 237);   **9.** E: the black dot is moving round the two verticals clockwise top/bottom/ bottom/top. The white dot is moving up and down the first vertical by half its length each time;   **10.** segment: it is a part, the rest are whole;   **11.** break, rake; **12.** £384. Harry's share is £240, ie each part is £48 (£240 ÷ 5). Therefore, the original amount was £48 × 8 (parts) (3 + 5) = £384;   **13.** C: looking across, the dot is moving from corner to corner clockwise. Looking down, it is moving from corner to corner anticlockwise;   **14.** lee crock = cockerel. The jobs/professions are: engineer = rein gene, mechanic = can chime, salesman = mean lass and attorney = no treaty;   **15.** 29: 52 + 64 = 116. 116 ÷ 4 = 29. Similarly 93 + 95 = 188. 188 ÷ 4 = 47;   **16.** E: in all the others all areas common to two circles are shaded. In E, one such area is not; **17.** titanic;   **18.** IJKON: the rest are in the sequence three consecutive letters of the alphabet, then miss a letter, then reverse the next two; **19.** 7462/2647;   **20.** A;   **21.** C: the rest are the same figure rotated;   **22.** vestigial, rudimentary;   **23.** READ, WORN;   **24.** 27: halve the second and third numbers then multiply the first three numbers in each line to produce the fourth number, so 9 × 3 (6 ÷ 2) × 1 (2 ÷ 2) = 27;   **25.** to fight shy of; **26.** C: A contains the same figures as E and B contains the same figures as D; **27.** 8: multiply the two outside numbers to obtain the number formed by the middle two digits reversed;   **28.** F: so that the first column is a mirror image of the third column and the second column is a mirror image of the fourth column;   **29.** affluent;   **30.** generalities;   **31.** 4 6 1 3 5 2 or 2 5 3 1 6 4;   **32.** H: the left-hand figure rotates 90 degrees clockwise and goes to the bottom. The right-hand figure rotates 90 degrees anticlockwise and goes to the top. The centre ellipse changes from black to white;   **33.** contemplate;   **34.** ignorant = no rating. The synonyms are erudite = rude tie, learned = dear Len and literate = elite art;   **35.** 5617: in all the others, the third digit is the difference between the first and second digits and the first digit is the difference between the third and fourth digits;   **36.** A: each line and column contains the main figure once reversed, a white dot, a black dot and the internal figure once reversed;   **37.** tyro;   **38.** HUMANELY;   **39.** 1: each triangle contains the digits 1–9 once each only; **40.** D: in each line and column ellipses are only carried forward to the third cloud when the same colour ellipse appears in the same position in the first two clouds; however, they then change from black to white and vice versa.

Test 14: Answers

1. D: each segment is a mirror image of the segment opposite; **2.** trip, jaunt; **3.** R: skip two letters then three, ie AbcDefgHijKlmnOpqR; **4.** 7, 8: looking down each column alternately, take the difference, then add, so, the difference between 2 and 9 = 7 and 5 + 3 = 8; **5.** D: so that the four arrows are pointing North, South, East, West and opposite pointers are the same type, ie finger or arrow; **6.** CRUDE, SUBTLE; **7.** premise; **8.** 21: pairs of numbers in lines reading across = 24; **9.** D: opposite corner blocks of four squares are identical; **10.** pillory; **11.** pleasant present; **12.** 1212: 6 × 2 = 12, 5 + 7 = 12. Similarly 4 × 6 = 24 and 9 + 7 = 16 (2416); **13.** C: the square on the left goes to the top, the square second left goes to middle right, the square second right goes to the bottom and the square on the right goes middle left; **14.** rod arch = orchard. The musical terms are baritone = no baiter, concerto = rent coco, overture = revue rot and rhapsody = shop yard; **15.** 2 in the left-hand square and 8 in the right-hand square. Each row of numbers in the left-hand square is multiplied by 2 to arrive at the row opposite in the right-hand square, ie 3967 × 2 = 7934; **16.** H: each row and column contains three black stars and four white stars; **17.** ON CLOUD NINE; **18.** Jill 30, Peter 40, Kate 50; **19.** to give a dog a bad name; **20.** C: all white segments remain the same but black segments turn white and flip over; **21.** 5: each number represents the number of times that a number is adjacent to it, either horizontally, vertically or diagonally; **22.** B: the contents of the third hexagon in each row and column are determined by the contents of the first two hexagons. Only when lines appear once in the same position in these two hexagons are they carried forward to the third hexagon; **23.** ADORE, CHERISH, VENERATE, REVERE; **24.** WITH ONE FELL SWOOP; **25.** E: work along the top row, then back along the second row etc, repeating the first three symbols; **26.** OPPOSITE, MATCHING; **27.** MUYJP = jumpy; **28.** 50 minutes; **29.** A: looking across and down, only when the same colour dot appears in the same position in the first two hexagons is it carried forward to the third hexagon, but then changes from white to black and vice versa; **30.** fanlight: it is a British-English term, the rest are American-English terms; **31.** F; **32.** 7 and 9: the numbers at the bottom are the sum of the digits of the connected numbers at the top; **33.** C: the taller triangle remains stationary. The other triangle moves from right to left by half the distance of the base of the taller triangle each time. The section common to both triangles is always shaded; **34.** breastbone; **35.** PENINSULA; **36.** Tony 42, Cherie 38, Gordon 56; **37.** 7: all the rest have a mirror-image pairing; **38.** artichoke = take choir. The animals are antelope = one leapt, elephant = the plane, panther = trap hen and gazelle = leg laze; **39.** 17: add the number of items together, which gives 83 + 77 + 62 + 95 = 317 among 100 women. This gives three items to each and four items to 17 of these women. The least number of women to have all three items is, therefore, 17;   **40.** B: the square moves from right to left, the ellipse rotates 90 degrees and goes from left to right and the dot moves to the extreme right within the ellipse.

Test 15: Answers

1. C: all the other figures are identical. In C the dot is in the wrong place;   **2.** Billy;   **3.** tit for tat;   **4.** 11: each pyramid of three numbers totals 21;   **5.** B: one rectangle remains stationary while the other rotates by half of the length of the stationary rectangle anticlockwise at each stage;   **6.** concerto: it is music written for instruments, the rest being songs, typically with words;   **7.** scale;   **8.** 32: (32 less 75 per cent = 8, less 0.625 = 3, less 1 = 2);   **9.** 17;   **10.** ineptitude;   **11.** contribution;   **12.** 2: the numbers surrounding each dot are always in ascending/descending order, eg 2467 or 7642;   **13.** E: the only one where a tail with a little circle is attached to a triangle;

14.

P	E	A	K		Z	E	A	L
	A		I		E			
	S		N	O	S	Y		V
S	T	A	G			T	A	M	E
U		T				W		T
C	O	O	L		U	N	D	O
H		M	A	I	N		A	
			M		I		R	
S	H	I	P		T	A	K	E

15. 8 3
       4 2

Start at the bottom left-hand square and work round the perimeter anticlockwise spiralling into the centre and repeating the numbers 38429;

16. D: so that looking round the octagon at segments in pairs, there are four identical pairs with black/white reversal;   **17.** cold;   **18.** 30 18 48 66. Starting at the top, add pairs of numbers in each column to arrive at the next number;   **19.** flippancy, levity;   **20.** A: the top and bottom figures fold down and up onto the line respectively;   **21.** C: in all the others each line across in the same position in each square contains the same three symbols, albeit in a different order;   **22.** man to man;   **23.** intricate;   **24.** 60 kg + one-sixth of its own weight = 72 kg; 46 kg + one-third of its own weight = 69 kg (ie, 69/3 = 23);   **25.** D;   **26.** retrograde: it means to worsen, the rest being to improve;   **27.** 22: there are two alternate sequences, the first increases by 2, 4, 8 etc and the second decreases by 4, 8, 16 etc;   **28.** long;   **29.** A: the combination of dots on the inside is the same as in the diamond directly opposite;   **30.** 3: reverse the numbers either side and divide. So, 75 (57) ÷ 25 (52) = 3;   **31.** EASTBOUND;   **32.** consequence;   **33.** D: all the others are identical. D contains a line in the wrong position;   **34.** 5: 5 × 18 = 90. 90 ÷ 2 = 45. Similarly 7 × 6 = 42. 42 ÷ 2 = 21;   **35.** past;   **36.** B: it contains the same shape of string but with large/small circle reversal;   **37.** 3: the numbers in the outside ring, top and bottom are arrived at by adding, ie 4 + 2 + 3 = 9 and 7 + 6 + 3 = 16. The numbers in the outside ring left and right are arrived at by multiplying, ie 4 × 7 × 3 = 84 and 2 × 6 × 3 = 36;   **38.** keen as mustard;   **39.** allegorical, factual;   **40.** E: the only one where an arrow points to a figure that has an odd number of sides.

Text 16: Answers

1. sure;   **2.** E: it contains a triangle in a circle, a circle in a square and a circle in a triangle;   **3.** ear, leg and rib, to make weary, elegy and tribe;   **4.** 5: add the first three numbers in each row, then divide by 3 to obtain the final number: 2 + 9 + 4 = 15/3 = 5;   **5.** transcend: all the other words relate to fall. Transcend is a word relating to rise;   **6.** B: the contents of the final square in each horizontal and vertical line is determined by the contents of the first two squares. Lines are carried forward from the first two squares to the final square, except where two lines appear in the same position, in which case they are cancelled out;   **7.** YIGEN = eying;   **8.** slight;   **9.** 2 mins 30 seconds ((3.5 + 0.25) × 60/90) minutes = 3.75 × 60/90 = 2.5 mins or 2 mins 30 secs;   **10.** silver;   **11.** E: the first four complete figures are being repeated in the same order but only the left half is shown;   **12.** 15. Add the top and left-hand numbers and divide by 4: 47 + 13 = 60/4 = 15;   **13.** hardly ever;   **14.** 5: looking down columns from left to right, 96 + 427 = 523;   **15.** F;   **16.** D: the rest are all the same figure rotated;   **17.** O. Start at A and jump to alternate segments working clockwise in the sequence: AbCdeFghiJklmnO;   **18.** summit, conference;   **19.** end: to give impend and endear;   **20.** rear;   **21.** d. like a pyramid;   **22.** merlin;   **23.** Be sure the brain is engaged before putting the mouth in gear;   **24.** Yoga: the first letter of each word is the same as the last letter of the preceding word; **25.** 38: $(8 \times 7 = 56) - (3 \times 4 = 12) = 44$; $(7 \times 9 = 63) - (4 \times 8 = 32) = 31$; $(5 \times 10 = 50) - (2 \times 6 = 12) = 38$;   **26.** By the time a man can read a woman like a book he is too old to collect a library;   **27.** C: each pair of circles is added together to produce the circle above, but similar symbols disappear;   **28.** 21; **29.** disgorge;   **30.** The first two letters start the name of a country and the last two letters finish the name: POLAND, TONGA, SENEGAL, FINLAND, JORDAN, SPAIN;   **31.** GIGANTIC;   **32.** 96: $(6 \times 5) + (2 \times 4) = 38$; $(6 \times 2) + (7 \times 7) = 61$; $(8 \times 7) + (5 \times 8) = 96$;   **33.** mullet, grilse;   **34.** A;   **35.** F: looking both across and down, only lines or dots that are common to the first two squares are carried forward to the third square;   **36.** carapace;   **37.** c. flower;   **38.** scarab;   **39.** LCA. The others make: flagon, fiacre, feline; **40.** bantam-weight.

Test 17: Answers

1. 11.27 am, ie 33 mins before 12 noon. $4 \times 33 = 132$ mins past 9 am = 11.12 am;   **2.** Ban(glad)esh;   **3.** boycott, proscribe;   **4.** B: each horizontal line contains one each of the three different left-hand, right-hand and middle portions;   **5.** 1792 steps (896×2);   **6.** temper, ermine, negate; **7.** chaste/chased;   **8.** D: the curved lines turn straight, and the straight lines turn curved;   **9.** astute;   **10.** HESITATE, RELATIVE;   **11.** TY. Read along the top lines, middle lines and bottom lines in each set respectively to spell out the words: solitude, dedicate and alacrity;   **12.** 99: $4 + 5 = 9$, $3 + 6 = 9$;   **13.** February;   **14.** kill two birds with one stone;   **15.** card: all the words in list A can be prefixed with 'red', all the words in list B can be prefixed with 'blue';   **16.** A: starting at the black circle the circles are in sets of five, which are being repeated, except that in each set of five the black circle moves up one space;   **17.** domains and aim; all the other words are in pairs so that each three-letter word is spelt backwards in the middle of one of the seven-letter words: precast/ace, panache/can, attempt/met, sadness/end, special/ice, presume/use, suburbs/rub. The word *domains* spells iam backwards, not aim;   **18.** 3: starting at the top, and reading clockwise, each number, formed by the top and bottom digits in that order, is the previous number plus the sum of its digits;   So, $12 + 1 + 2 = 15$, $15 + 1 + 5 = 21$;   **19.** uniform;   **20.** A: C and D are the same with black and white reversed, as are B and E;   **21.** c. a sail;   **22.** A: the figure at the bottom rotates 90 degrees and goes to the left. The figure at the top rotates

180 degrees and goes inside the figure now on the left. The figure in the middle rotates 90 degrees and goes to the right;   **23.** D;   **24.** desserts (or 'stressed' anticlockwise);   **25.** beagle, barbet;   **26.** 145. Each number is obtained by adding the previous four numbers;   **27.** C;   **28.** d. steak; **29.** The most brilliantly dressed army will usually lose;   **30.** Each word has three letters in succession in the alphabet;   **31.** night;   **32.** (40; 4 × 7 = 28) + (9 × 2 = 18) = 46; (7 × 3 = 21) + (8 × 4 = 32) = 53; (5 × 6 = 30) + (2 × 5 = 10) = 40;   **33.** perishable;   **34.** D;   **35.** D: opposite segments are a mirror image of each other, but with black/ white reversal;   **36.** pedestal; **37.** plaice;   **38.** a. brougham;   **39.** industrial revolution;   **40.** harridan.

Test 18: Answers

1. A: directly opposite squares are a mirror image of each other;   **2.** 10: each number on the outside is the sum of the two numbers in the middle ring adjacent to it, plus the number in the centre. So, 4 + 3 + 3 = 10; **3.** NO SLAM = salmon. The dogs are: looped = poodle; bag eel = beagle; sail UK = saluki; and bastes = basset;   **4.** manners: all words can be prefixed with *table*;   **5.** E: the sequence appears looking across each row of circles in the ellipses. The top row alternates right-sloping stripes, left-sloping stripes etc, the middle row is repeating the first three circles, and in the bottom row, the black segment is moving one segment clockwise at each stage; **6.** out of this world;   **7.** brow;   **8.** all hands on deck;   **9.** 569 and 986: all the others are in anagram pairs of numbers, 749/479, 682/268, 516/165, 382/238, 578/758 and 129/291;   **10.** air, to give fair, hair, pair, chair and flair;   **11.** D: the figures on the outside transfer to the inside and change shape and colour. So, a white circle on the outside becomes a black triangle on the inside;   **12.** a. hard white mineral;   **13.** 3: 39 + 72 = 111, 21 + 16 = 37, 111 ÷ 37 = 3;   **14.** D: the contents of each hexagon are determined by the contents of the two hexagons immediately below it. Where two identical circles appear in the same corner in these two hexagons, they are carried forward to the hexagon above but change from black to white and vice versa;   **15.** conducted tour;   **16.** schism, rift;   **17.** edacious, generous; **18.** 1: so that the total of each vertical line of numbers increases by one each time;   **19.** clog;   **20.** curt;   **21.** c. gown;   **22.** $1^{47}/_{81}$ (× $1^1/_3$);   **23.** beauty;   **24.** papillon;   **25.** 69: (6 × 9 = 54) +(7 × 8 = 56) = 110; (2 × 7 = 14) + (9 × 11 = 99) = 113; (5 × 3 = 15) + (6 × 9 = 54) = 69;   **26.** jackal, alpaca;   **27.** E: the symbols in the lower two circles combine to form the circle above, but similar symbols disappear;   **28.** d. a ranch;   **29.** William Tell Jr had headaches;   **30.** c. ignorant;   **31.** $1^{115}/_{128}$ (× 1.5);   **32.** D. The others are: a. torque, b. toucan, c. toupee;   **33.** protract, lengthen; **34.** A;   **35.** B: the figures are mirror-images but with black/white reversal;

36. C: so that each adjoining pair of hexagons contains three black dots and five white dots;   **37.** d. (hockey). The others are: marine, anchor, beacon, piracy;   **38.** 13¼. There are two series: +1¾ and −1¾: 8, 9¾, 11½, 13¼ and 10, 8¼, 6½;   **39.** lengthways;   **40.** southerly.

Test 19: Answers

1. 12;   **2.** flower: this is the whole thing, the rest are parts of a flower; **3.** 49, 46, 47, 44. Look at pairs of lines: 7 + 9 = 16, 4 + 9 = 13, 9 + 2 = 11, 7 + 2 = 9. Therefore, 22 + 24 = 46, 20 + 24 = 44, 24 + 25 = 49, 22 + 25 = 47; **4.** quail;   **5.** new clue;   **6.** C: so that each straight line of three hexagons contains one each of the three different symbols;   **7.** tiny magical alarm; **8.** 80: each number is formed by multiplying the number formed by the first two digits of the previous number by its third digit. So, 16 × 5 = 80;   **9.** signs of the zodiac;   **10.** principal, subsidiary;   **11.** F: the contents of the last square in each row and column is determined by the contents of the first two squares. Only when the same figure appears in the same position is a figure carried forward to the final square, in which case two circles become a trapezium, and two trapeziums become a circle;   **12.** 5 and 14: each number represents a letter of the alphabet according to its numerical position in the alphabet. The letters in each column spell out three letter numbers: 1, 2, 6 and 10;   **13.** weaponless: all the other words contain the adjacent letters ONE;

14.

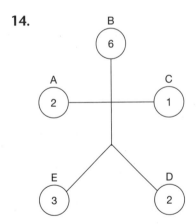

In each figure, A + C = E, A + C + E = B, B/E = D;

15. founder;   16. R: the letter on the outside is positioned midway between its two adjacent letters on the inside, in the alphabet;   17. XYZ = OLD: oldest, folded, scolds, uphold;   18. B: the outer arc moves 90° clockwise at each stage, the middle arc moves 180° at each stage, the inner arc moves 180° at each stage;   19. waspish, peppery;   20. 48 mph. Say the journey takes 120 miles. The first half of the journey (60 miles) takes 60/40 = 1.5 hours; the second half takes 60/60 = 1.0 hour. So, the journey of 120 miles takes 1.5 + 1.0 = 2.5 hours and therefore, the average speed is 120/2.5 = 48 mph;   21. MICROSCOPE;   22. badger;   23. a. iron bucket;   24. midge, the others start with a fish: bass, sole, dab, brill, cod, carp;   25. cuckoo, chough;   26. wheels within wheels;   27. IB;   28. hard;   29. The dimmer the light the greater the scandal;   30. a. bird;   31. a. tctale = cattle. The others are: canary, merlin, puffin, peewit;

32.   63. Multiply opposites:

4 × 3 = 12	1 × 6 = 6	6 × 7 = 42
2 × 6 = 12	2 × 4 = 8	1 × 3 = 3
7 × 9 = 63	7 × 8 = 56	2 × 9 = 18
Total: 87	70	63

33. eggplant;   34. C;   35. Two letters can be placed at the beginning to make a new word: abalone, behold, changer, damask, enforce;   36. peculiar;   37. trochlea;   38. They all contain the name of a tree: ash, elm, oak, lime, plum;   39. endanger, preserve;   40. 25.

Test 20: Answers

1. 105 kg; 250 × 0.7 × 0.8 × 0.75;   2. advocacy;   3. rambling: the rest are all anagrams of each other;   4. 3: the rest all have a mirror image pair, 1/9, 2/11, 4/12, 5/10, 6/14, 7/15, 8/13;   5. 248: in the rest there is the same difference between each digit, eg 8 (–3) 5 (–3) 2;   6. Tuesday;   7. A: black segments only appear in the final square in each row and column when they appear in the same position in the first two squares;   8. ruminate;   9. Their last four letters spell out another word reading backwards; groom/moor, spank/knap, plaid/dial, breve/ever;   10. C: it contains one figure which has been inverted and cannot be rotated to look the same;   11. 4725: delete the digits outside the brackets that appear twice, and insert the remaining digits in the brackets in the same order that they appear outside the brackets – 8418 (4725) 1725;   12. circle;   13. cranberry, to give arc, sir, pea, can, rub, ode, for, mar, coy;   14. desperado;   15. Measu(re For M)easure;   16. be all and end all;   17. obdurate, amenable;   18. C: each triangle changes from black to white in turn. At each stage a new triangle is added moving anticlockwise, and this

new triangle first of all appears black, then alternates black/white at each stage;   **19.** bream, cod, salmon;   **20.** 16 at the top, 10,920 at the bottom. The top number is the sum of all the digits in the previous diamond (1 + 3 + 8 + 4 + 0). The bottom number is the product of the two numbers in the previous diamond (13 × 840);   **21.** 21534 or 43512. Note that the sum of the numbers 1–5 is 15. According to the first line of the question, the numbers 2 and 4 must, therefore, be in the outside circles;   **22.** scarlet: the other words all carry an animal in reverse: elk, ram, dog, cat, rat;   **23.** $^{7}/648$ (x $- ^{1}/3$);   **24.** b. pumpkin;   **25.** knockabout;   **26.** No matter which way you ride, it is always up hill and against the wind every time, just bad luck; **27.** A: the two circles below combine to produce the circle above, but similar symbols disappear;   **28.** incite, calm;   **29.** Fools rush in where fools have been before;   **30.** E: so that the dot can be placed in the circle and the triangle only;   **31.** Vatrac (cravat). The others are: willow, spruce, acacia, deodar; **32.** THIEVISH, CRIMINAL;   **33.** CROOK;   **34.** E;   **35.** cabal, junta;   **36.** C: only black dots from the circles and white dots from the squares are carried forward to the hexagon;   **37.** Chaplin. The others are: Carter, Hoover, Truman, Wilson;   **38.** bonanza;   **39.** mildness, rigidity;   **40.** 4: (13 – 7 = 6) × (8 – 6 = 2) = 12; (9 – 5 = 4) × (7 – 3 = 4) = 16; (9 – 8 = 1) × (7 – 3 = 4) = 4.

Test 21: Answers

1. E: it only contains four small white circles whereas the rest contain five; **2.** 28;   **3.** kidney;   **4.** quatrain: it is connected with the number four, whilst the rest all have a connection with the number five;   **5.** pose, model; **6.** T: the letters in the middle convert the verb around the outside into past tense: come/came, know/knew, send/sent;   **7.** 16;   **8.** 871: 65/50 × 670; **9.** badger, monkey, rabbit. The missing letters can be arranged to spell out *bribed men*;

10.

¹S	²H	Y	³D	E	W
A	⁴O	N	I	O	⁵N
⁶L	A	U	G	⁷H	I
O	⁸X	⁹E	N	O	N
¹⁰N	E	W	E	L	J
¹¹O	W	E	¹²P	E	A

11. C: the contents of the third circle in each row and column is determined by the contents of the previous two circles. Only when black or white dots appear in the same position in each of these two circles are they carried forward to the third circle, but then change from black to white and vice versa;   **12.** 10: in each row and column the difference between alternate digits is the same, ie 16 – 10 = 10 – 4;   **13.** forest florist;   **14.** BE TASK = basket. The ships are, in order: tanker, galley, launch, sampan;   **15.** bundle of laughs;   **16.** C: the left-hand portion is folded over onto the right-hand portion;   **17.** hearsay, rumour;   **18.** 8612: all the other numbers have their digits in descending order;   **19.** tender loving care;   **20.** act your age;   **21.** B: if you draw a line down the centre to divide the set of pentagons into two halves, the right half is a mirror image of the left half;   **22.** FRONT;   **23.** D;   **24.** vicuna;   **25.** C. A is murmur; B is mumble; D is mulish;   **26.** ORTHODOX, SECEDING;   **27.** E: x is added to y to make z; 1 is added to 2 to make 3, but like symbols disappear;   **28.** times: the other words also make words when spelt backwards;   **29.** hilltops;   **30.** b. a ballet movement;   **31.** Y, Z: the letters are made with three straight lines;   **32.** YASHMAKS;   **33.** IMMODEST, INDECENT;   **34.** E;   **35.** When the bell rings there had better be some supper;   **36.** London. The others are: Scilly, Penang, Orkney, Cayman;   **37.** ALKALI;   **38.** MACARONI;   **39.** 8: (9 + 7 + 1 = 17) – (4 + 3 = 7) = 10; (8 + 5 + 6 = 19) – (7 + 2 = 9) = 10; (5 + 8 + 2 = 15) – (6 + 1 = 7) = 8;   **40.** FEEBLENESS.

Test 22: Answers

1. D: each circle in the bottom half is a repeat of a circle in the top half, but rotated 90° clockwise;   **2.** SEEK, SEED, FEED, FEND, FIND. Some variations are possible and allowable;   **3.** adroit;

4. agent:

ALIGHT (AGENT) BONNET
1   2   5   1 2 3 4 5   4 3

5. 10: starting from the bottom and working to the top, each triangular group of three numbers totals 21;   **6.** O: opposite letters are the same number of letters from the beginning and end of the alphabet respectively;   **7.** B: so that each row and column contains one each of the three different symbols;

8. The number of votes received by the winning candidate was (93648 + 25627 + 10681 + 5924) divided by 4 = 33970.

	33970
The second received 33970 – 5924 =	28046
The third received 33970 – 10681 =	23289
The fourth received 33970 – 25627 =	8343
Total	93648

9. HA: take the numerical position of each letter in the alphabet to reveal the sequence of consecutive square numbers 1, 4, 9, 16, 25, 36, 49, 64, 81; **10.** gilt: *dart, send* is an anagram of *stranded*; *dine, gilt* is an anagram of *diligent*; **11.** H; **12.** E: the rectangle rotates 90°, the parallelogram flips over and goes inside the rectangle and the ellipse rotates 90° and goes below the rectangle; **13.** lap; **14.** 7: add the numbers in the same segments of the first two circles to obtain the numbers in the same segments in the third circle. So, 3 + 5 = 8, 2 + 7 = 9, 4 + 3 = 7; **15.** experimental: add the letters e, m and n; **16.** d. open to all; **17.** go like hot cakes; **18.** bilk, swindle; **19.** 9: add the top line of numbers to the bottom line to obtain the middle line, ie 473892 + 516359 = 990251; **20.** B: there are two alternate sequences. In the first, the hexagon is losing one side at a time, in the other the hexagon is being constructed one line at a time; **21.** b. hassock; **22.** A cluttered desk a man of genius; **23.** d. loop of thread; **24.** HORRIBLE, SHOCKING; **25.** Inland Revenue; **26.** knothole; **27.** 2C; **28.** sheldrake; **29.** 4: take the Roman numeral value of the second/third letters: AVIATOR; FIXTURE; WIZARDS; DIVERSE; **30.** willow;

31. 0.10. There are two series: –0.19 and +0.19:

(–0.19) 0.67, 0.48, 0.29, 0.10
(+0.19) 0.69, 0.88, 1.07, 1.26

32. PARAGRAPHS; **33.** RESTRAIN, WITHHOLD; **34.** E; **35.** d. skiing; **36.** 23: the third line is the first line of figures reversed. The fourth line is the second line of figures reversed; **37.** A; **38.** El Salvador (an anagram of lover, salad as Bangladesh is an anagram of blade, gnash); **39.** importance;

40. 11. Opposite numbers are deducted then added:

6 – 1 = 5	8 – 3 = 5	7 – 3 = 4
7 – 2 = 5	4 – 2 = 2	9 – 7 = 2
9 – 3 = 6 +	9 – 1 = 8 +	6 – 1 = 5 +
16	15	11

Test 23: Answers

1. D: the black triangle affixes itself to each arm in turn, the white triangle moves backwards and forwards between two positions, the triangle with the dot moves to each end of the middle arm (above then below) in turn, and the circle moves clockwise to each internal corner in turn;   **2.** 8 kg: 16/2 = 8;   **3.** highland;   **4.** intricate, simple;

5.

A T I		
M B E M Y C I G H		
T O E A A M W E M O O O		
F N X R T O I F E D O L		

The word *melodramatic* is spelt out round the outside perimeter;

6. D: the others are all the same figure rotated;

7. In 12 months' time;

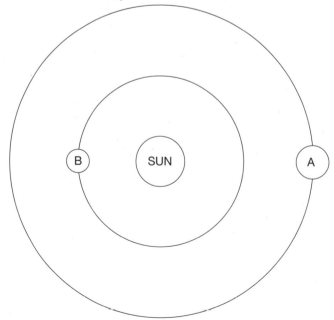

8. take the bull by the horns; **9.** A: large circles turn to small, and vice versa; **10.** E: so that each line of letters produces an anagram of a colour: amber, green, azure, lemon; **11.** 10: each two-figure number is the sum of the digits of one of the three-figure numbers in the opposite circle; **12.** Desdemona, to give: mid, ace, was, had, hue, him, who, ban, sea; **13.** D: the figure rotates 90° at each stage and a different portion is shaded in turn; **14.** at the ready; **15.** aboriginal; **16.** 16: 12 + 16 = 28/7 = 4; **17.** banana, lemon, orange; **18.** identical twins; **19.** ch(ape)l; **20.** satisfactory: add the letters i, f, t and r; **21.** leaf; **22.** shortage; **23.** 4: from the top, 7 × 28 = 196 and from the bottom, 4 × 49 = 196;

24. 9 kg.   LH: 6 kg × 6 = 36 kg   RH: 5 kg × 5 = 25 kg
                     4 kg × 4 = 16 kg   9 kg × 3 = 27 kg
                     36 + 16 = 52 kg   25 + 27 = 52 kg

25. AEROBATICS; **26.** LAZINESS, SLOWNESS; **27.** E: x is added to y to make z,1 is added to 2 to make 3, but similar symbols disappear; **28.** b. pyramid (it is a solid, the rest are polygons); **29.** irritant; **30.** b. boat; **31.** +12. There are two series: +5 and –9. –3, +2, +7, +12, +6, –3, –12; **32.** 2: 4 × 10 = 40 and 23 + 15 = 38; **33.** TIMOROUS, FEARLESS; **34.** C; **35.** d. sugar; **36.** beetle; **37.** bridge; the others are: eggcup, juicer, grater, scales; **38.** Trust everybody but always cut the cards; **39.** cardinal; **40.** WORKADAY.

Test 24: Answers

1. 330 and 41. Multiply the two numbers of the previous pair together to obtain the top number, and add the same two numbers to get the bottom number. So, 30 × 11 = 330, 30 + 11 = 41; **2.** intrinsic: it is necessary because it is something that forms an essential part of a whole; the rest are necessary as a duty; **3.** 75: 5 × 75 = 375. Similarly 7 × 52 = 364; **4.** D: in all the others a black circle is in the middle of the chain of three connected circles; **5.** temperature; **6.** wary, rash; **7.** past; **8.** OPPORTUNE: add the letters p and u; **9.** NFOLE = felon;

10.

¹A	D	²R	O	I	³T
⁴C	H	O	P	⁵A	A
⁶T	A	L	⁷A	S	P
⁸M	⁹D	E	S	K	¹⁰A
U	O	¹¹B	I	N	D
¹²D	E	M	A	N	D

11. B; it has lateral symmetry, in other words if the square was cut from top to bottom down the middle, the two halves (left and right) would be identical; **12.** 3: the numbers in successive triangles add up to 8, 9, 10, 11, 12, 13; **13.** skeleton; **14.** foolish: all the other words start and finish with consecutive letters of the alphabet, eg *carried*; **15.** speculator; **16.** D: the figures are in the same order around the body; **17.** O and H. There are two sequences going from top to bottom of the columns as follows: AbCdeFghiJklmnO, and ZyxWvutSrqpoNmlkjiH; **18.** TA101: substitute Roman numerals for numbers to read: red, lime, navy, gold and blue. TA101 spells TAXI (10 = X and I = 1); **19.** 88: 8 × 1 = 8, 8 + 0 = 8; **20.** B: reverse each line and discard the third figure from the end each time; **21.** c. a heap of stones; **22.** They all commence with a boy's name: Bart, Tim, Pat, Don, Alf; **23.** B: reversing the first analogy, the four black squares become one white square in the centre with four arms attached to it; **24.** week, day, year; **25.** 34: the first column is multiplied by the third column, and the second column deducted: (5 × 7) − 1 = 34; **26.** ADVOCATE, ATTORNEY; **27.** D. The lower circles' symbols combine to form the circle above, but similar symbols disappear; **28.** c. fumerole; **29.** All work and no play means you make money hand over fist; **30.** winnow; **31.** b. silk handkerchief; **32.** a state of confusion; **33.** 84: (7 × 4) × 9/3 = 84; (6 × 8) × 10/5 = 96; (3 × 7) × 8/2 = 84; **34.** B; **35.** RUBLEO (rouble). The others are: earwig, scarab, tsetse, hornet; **36.** $1^7/_8$ (+$^1/_2$); **37.** dahlia; **38.** mere;

39.

17	6	12	8	22
24	13	14	9	5
11	7	1	25	21
3	23	18	19	2
10	16	20	4	15

40. grudgingly.

Test 25: Answers

1. D: the figure is rotating 45° clockwise at each stage; **2.** 40 minutes, or 11.20 am; **3.** cohesive; **4.** erect, supine; **5.** B: at each stage the black element moves clockwise, first by one space, then two, then three, etc; **6.** vicuna: it is a natural material, the rest are man-made; **7.** soul/sole; **8.** selling dwelling; **9.** C: the top bit folds down into the square, and the bottom bit folds up into it; **10.** 15: start at 0 and jump two segments each time clockwise in the sequence: 0 (+ 1) 1 (+ 2) 3 (+ 3) 6 (+ 4) 10 (+ 5) 15 (+ 6) 21; **11.** like a cat on a hot tin roof; **12.** evaporate: add the letters v and t; **13.** A: only dots which appear twice in the same segment in the previous three circles are carried forward; **14.** filament; **15.** 941319: in all the others the first two digits are added together to obtain the third and fourth digits, and the second digit is added to the third and fourth digits to obtain the fifth and sixth digits. For example, with 681422, 6 + 8 = 14 + 8 = 22; **16.** spinach, carrot, bean; **17.** JLM: in all the others there are two spaces in the alphabet between the first two letters and no space between the last two, eg AbcDE; **18.** $65^2 = 16^2 + 63^2$; **19.** reduce, cereal, allure; **20.** megastar; **21.** E: in all the others, the number of sides on the figure in the middle is one less than the number of sides on the figure on the outside; **22.** platform; **23.** bubble; **24.** a. dog; **25.** scatterbrain; **26.** DUMBSTRUCK; **27.** 2C; **28.** METEORIC; **29.** IRON; **30.** BUTTER. The others are: mohair, sateen, damask, calico; **31.** It won't work. Read the letter between the letters which follow: ie, H (i) JMZPS (t) UCAIV (w); **32.** C. The others are: malice, makeup, makers; **33.** IMPOSING, SPLENDID; **34.** C; **35.** c. opaque; **36.** felicity, bliss; **37.** thinly sliced cabbage; **38.** b. mixture; **39.** GRIEVOUS, MOURNFUL; **40.** shortbread.